Unstoppable Referrals

HOW TO GET 10X MORE REFERRALS WITH
HALF THE EFFORT

Steve Gordon

Unstoppable CEO Press
TALLAHASSEE, FLORIDA, USA

Unstoppable CEO Press
PO Box 16334
Tallahassee, FL, 32317, United States
UnstoppableCEO.net

Ordering Information:
Quantity sales. Special discounts are available on quantity purchases by corporations, associations, and others. For details, contact the "Special Sales Department" at the address above.

Unstoppable referrals/ Steve Gordon. —1st ed.

ISBN 978-0-9904941-0-2

Praise for Unstoppable Referrals

"This book will radically change the way referrals are done."

When Steve asked me to review this one, I was concerned. Why would he ask an internet marketer to review his book on offline business referrals? Because he's a freaking genius, that's why! <u>*I learned (through wonderfully readable prose, by the way) that results online can be exploded using Steve's simple but effective techniques.*</u> *His simple system turns the whole concept of referrals upside down and shakes out the good stuff.*

This book will radically change the way referrals are done, and that would be a good thing.
- *Steven Washer, Chief Education Officer, BrainyVideo.com*

"The first new thinking on referrals in decades."

The truth is that most people feel very uncomfortable asking for referrals, and most people you ask feel uncomfortable giving them. The only advice that trainers and writers seem to have on this is to ask more often. Unfortunately, that just doesn't cut it.

*Steve's book and system, Unstoppable Referrals is the first to tackle the issue head on and to give a **simple, reliable method for getting referrals on a large scale without feeling salesy doing so**, and without making the people you ask feel pressured or uncomfortable. In fact, Steve shows you how to strengthen your relationship with them through the referral process.*

The system Steve shares is simple, it's step-by-step. And if you put the work into it, it will deliver results.

If you only ever buy one book on referrals, this is the one to get".
- *Ian Brodie, Bestselling Author of Email Persuasion*

*"This book provides the knowledge needed
to add <u>millions</u> to the bottom line."*

*"This book will quickly become a "must read" for any serious busi-
ness person. It is an easy read that distills Steve's extensive
knowledge and experience in getting business referrals.*

*Easy to understand, this book provides the knowledge needed to add
millions to the bottom line. Within 24 hours of reading I'd started to
implement the advice Steve gives and saw results right away."*

*- Stefan Drew, "The Marketing Magician", Author of Advertising
Secrets: Essential Advertising Tips That
Advertising Sales Reps Prefer You NOT To Know*

"I'm going to read it again and do exactly what he says."

*"Steve Gordon isn't merely one of a herd. No. Steve studies. Then he
calculates. Then he dives in and gets dirty and bruised from first-
hand experience. And as a result, he conquers.*

*That's how he's mastered the topic of generating referrals. And in
this book he's distilled down its most simple essence how you, too, can
build a steady, consistent, predictable flow of high quality referrals. I'm going to read it again and do exactly what he says."*

- Dov Gordon, The Alchemist Entrepreneur, DovGordon.net

*"Anyone interested in generating more referrals...
needs to read this book."*

"*Anyone interested in generating more referrals for their business needs to read this book. Steve Gordon provides clear examples and an easy-to-follow process that any business owner can use to produce significantly more referrals.*"

- *Michael Zipursky, CEO, ConsultingSuccess.com*

*"You must buy this book but when you do,
make sure you keep it out of sight from your competitors!"*

"*This book arrived across my desk on a very busy day. I had lots of other things to do but I thought I'd just read the first few pages just to check it was worth reading. About two hours later I am still reading it and I can't put it down. I've never seen such a well thought out process for making the whole thing run on steroids! Steve's book takes you step by step though creating your own highly responsive referral process. Throughout the journey, he litters the book with lots of golden nuggets of information. This is a book packed with information and advice. There's no messing around with pages of waffle. It's right to the point. You must buy this book but when you do, make sure you keep it out of sight from your competitors!*"

- *Mike Seddon, Internet Jetstream*

Contents

To Erin

Nothing in this world can take the place of persistence. Talent will not: nothing is more common than unsuccessful men with talent. Genius will not: unrewarded genius is almost a proverb. Education will not: the world is full of educated derelicts. Persistence and determination alone are omnipotent.

—CALVIN COOLIDGE

The Real Reason You're Not Getting All The Referrals You Should

Here's why you should read this book: The methods I'm about to share with you produce results...*fast*. In my own business I have generated as many as 248 referrals in a single week.

More typically, my clients who have applied these methods are often astonished at how immediately and easily they begin to attract 5 or 10 or 20 quality referrals in a single meeting with a client, who had never before referred.

There is a reason you're not getting all the referrals you think you should get. In this book I'll show you what that reason is and what to do to overcome it. Before we get there it's important that you know how I discovered the reason and how it acts as a barrier to a free and abundant flow of referrals.

In 2012, after studying the available wisdom on developing referrals, and after building two businesses on the strength of referrals, I decided to teach a seminar to business owners on cultivating referrals.

It was, as you might imagine, a hot topic. Over the course of several seminars, I taught a few hundred business owners and sales professionals the distilled knowledge about getting more referrals.

All the conventional information boiled down to two things:

#1. Ask more often.

#2. Develop deeper relationships through consistent follow-up.

Both principles are absolutely true, and both work. I've employed them throughout my business-building journey with success.

Several months after my seminars I met individually with 20 attendees. To my great disappointment, none of them had implemented the recommendations I'd taught. And none had seen any improvement in their referral business.

Each person admitted that they believed without a doubt that the actions I'd recommended would help them attract more referral business, yet they'd chosen not to act.

I started to press those I met in later meetings to understand why, if given the solution to their business problem, had they not acted. Again and again, I heard an answer that sounded like this:

> "I know it will work, I just don't feel comfortable asking so often. It feels like I'm being greedy. After all, that client just hired me and paid me. And I'm asking for something more. I've done a really good job, and if they appreciate it, they'll tell people."

The bottom line—these business people were avoiding asking for referrals because they felt uncomfortable.

They knew they were taking from the relationship and it put them at odds with their normal beliefs and practices.

At the same time, I was a member of, and leader in Business Networking International (BNI)—a strong contact networking group designed to create profitable referral relationships between member businesses.

In this group, members expressed difficulty in finding referrals for other members. Especially in what I call "hard-to-refer" businesses (those that require enormous trust to support a transaction).

As I probed, again the root cause became clear—members were uncomfortable making the referral in those high-trust areas.

So if we know the proven mechanism for getting more referrals (ask more and follow-up to build referral relationships), yet we're not doing it because it makes us act in conflict with our underlying belief systems (expressed as "being uncomfortable"), how then, can we expect to exert any influence over referrals in our business?

Uncovering The Root Cause

If we deconstruct what happens when a referral is made, it becomes clear why so many otherwise smart business people have such a fundamental problem asking for referrals.

If you and I are friends and I take my wife to a fabulous dinner at a great new restaurant in town, it's easy for me to share that experience with you and refer the restaurant.

For you to go to the restaurant, there's really no risk (sure you might get a meal you don't like, but other than being out $100, there's not much downside). You also know what the buying process will look like when you get there. You'll be seated at a table, be given a menu with prices on it and choose the items you want from the menu without pressure from the waiter (the *salesperson*).

But let's look at a different type of transaction. Let's imagine that we're again having a friendly conversation and I tell you how pleased I am to have just purchased a $1,000,000 whole life insurance policy. And I tell you that I'd like to introduce you to my life insurance salesperson.

Your reaction (unless you know you have an immediate need for a policy) is to start looking over your shoulder for the door.

And, I've likely put a strain on our relationship. Here's why...

I've asked you to take a sales meeting with a salesperson you do not know. Because I've shared my own satisfaction and joy over buying my $1,000,000 life insurance policy, the implication is that you should want one, too.

If you reject the purchase, you are, in a small way, rejecting me. And you don't want to do that...you don't even want to be in a position to do that. But it goes further.

If you agree to the introduction, you are, in your mind, agreeing to participate in a sales meeting. We both know it. And sales meetings come with sales pressure. You don't want either.

Unless you perceive a real and present need for a life insurance policy you may actually react as though I've overstepped my acceptable social boundary by trying to setup a meeting.

If you think any of this is overblown, think carefully about your own experiences as *the referral*—the person being referred.

Now, let's look at this dynamic from the side of the *referrer*—the person making the introduction—in our little scenario, I'm the referrer and you are the referral.

I know that there is great social risk to me in attempting to make this introduction. I already know that you might perceive my gesture as imposing. As the intermediary these are treacherous waters. I have huge downside risk from any number of factors. Yet, the only potential benefit I might receive is increased social capital from the referral and the salesperson, IF the match is a success.

Otherwise, my name is MUD with both of you.

And that brings me back to you, as business person, wanting more referrals, yet too uncomfortable to ask as often as you should.

You know that all of the social dynamic I describe exists and is real. And you know that when you ask a client to give you a referral or make an introduction, you place them in a difficult and uncomfortable position.

So you, and millions of business people like you, avoid the situation all together and simply allow the referrals to happen or not, without your intervention.

A Dangerous Game We Play

Leaving the flow of referrals into your business to chance is a dangerous game. Most often, business owners believe that if they simply provide great service, that referrals will come on their own.

To a degree, that's true. But they often come at such low volume and with such inconsistency that they cannot be relied upon as a primary source of new clients.

Yet, go to virtually any meeting with 2 or more business owners in the room and ask them where they get most of their business and they'll tell you—"word of mouth"—referrals.

Ask the next, more important question: "What are you doing to stimulate referrals?" And most will say, "Nothing."

In fact, in preparation for his book *The Referral Engine*, author John Jantsch surveyed several thousand business owners. He found two things:

#1. 63.4% felt that over half of their business came from referrals.

#2. 79.9% said they had no system of any kind to generate referrals.

Yet we all know referrals, when they make it to us in the right context, are the best customers. They buy with less effort than prospects that come from cold advertising.

According to a Nielsen study, prospects are four-times more likely to buy when referred.

But only 20% of businesses are doing anything proactive to get more referrals—all because the mechanism for getting them, that has been taught for the last 100 years is based on getting you to do something that makes you uncomfortable.

There's a Better, Faster Way to 10x More Referrals...and You Won't Have to Send Anyone to a Sales Meeting

I've spent the last 2-years perfecting a method for attracting referrals, while, at the same time, removing the underlying sales pressure created by the old methods.

This book is a blueprint you can use, starting today, to *attract* referrals and referral partners by delivering extreme value in advance. You'll remove the stress and social pressure of traditional referrals by significantly lowering the bar at the start of each new referral relationship. And you'll see how to use the by-product of this method to systematically turn referred prospects into clients.

I look forward to hearing your success story soon! Please send me a note at Steve@UnstoppableCEO.net and tell me how you've done.

Now, before you jump into the book, I want to alert you to the additional resources available to you beginning on Page 133. Most important among them is "The Unstoppable CEO™ Online" –The Daily Business Intelligence for Growing Businesses. In it, you'll get up to date insights on the topics covered in this book and the latest "what's working now" information on attracting great clients. To get it, go now to Unstoppable-CEO.net/online.

Part One:
The Essential Conditions Necessary For Attracting Referrals

CHAPTER 1

Are You Referable?

> **Download The Referability Assessment Tool**
> and use it while you read this chapter
>
> UnstoppableCEO.net/ReferralResources

Before we begin looking at how to get more referrals, it's important to understand what it is that makes you referable. Why would someone tell another person about your business? If you stop to think about it, it's a huge challenge to overcome.

The truth is, most don't refer. And they don't refer because, frankly, they don't care about you or your business. I know that's harsh, but we've got to face the truth. Clients don't care about your business, they care about their problem...and how you solve it. Referral partners don't care about your business. They have their own business to grow.

It's not that the world is cold and bleak and people are indifferent (although in some cases this is true). Most don't refer because it's simply not in their self-interest. And that's your fault and mine. We haven't engineered the business in a way that makes it a benefit for our clients and referral partners to introduce us.

Shame on us...we'll fix it in this book.

To do so, we need to understand exactly how you become referable. To get any referral four things must exist:

You're Different

If you want referrals, you've got to start by being different. There's no reason to talk about your business if you're just like every other competitor. This book will show you, very specifically, a formula for being different. When you're different, there's something to talk about. There's something noteworthy. Be different.

You're Valuable

To be referable, you've got to be valuable. Valuable to clients because you solve an important problem for them. Valuable to referral partners because you make them look good. And valuable to referrals, before the sale, because you give them knowledge and hope for a solution to a "bleeding-neck" problem. In Part 3, you'll discover how to be massively valuable to referral partners and their referrals. And in Part 4, we'll extend that to clients and their referrals.

You're Likeable

Look, if they don't like you, they're not referring you. It helps to be nice. (If you've got a sales force, this one's really important. After all, YOU may be likable, but if Sam the Salesman is a jerk, you're not getting referred.)

You're Trustworthy

Referrals are, essentially, a transfer of trust. Some of the trust the client or referral partner has in you is transferred to the person being referred. The process laid out in this book is designed to systematically build trust in clients, referral partners and, importantly, in the referred prospects themselves.

Now let's look at the three areas of your business that you can innovate to make you more referable.

Your Product/Service

It's possible to bake referability into your product or service. Facebook is a fabulous example...to make the product work, you've got to invite your friends. But it's not a particularly useful example if you're a builder or an attorney or small manufacturer or any "real-world" business.

UnstoppableCEO.net

You may be able to create a highly referable product or service. There are two approaches that work.

The first is to create a unique, custom product. Easy for a custom builder or certain types of manufacturers, but not easy for most businesses.

The second is to build such great quality into your product or service that it's unique and worth talking about. This is the more common approach..."If we do great work, people will spread the word." While this is true, it relies on the thoughtfulness, generosity and willingness of your clients to talk about you and what you've done for them. It leaves your client in the driver's seat on referrals and you're simply sitting back waiting, hoping they'll do their part and make your phone ring.

A dangerous place to be if that's your only referral tool, or worse, it's your only means of getting new clients.

The day will come when the clients don't do their part. And the phone doesn't ring...and you'll never see it coming.

Your Process

The second area that you might innovate to make you referable is your process. The way in which you interact with people in your business. For a service business, this can be a very powerful way to create an experience for people to talk about.

Starbucks, the biggest small business built almost exclusively by referral, did this masterfully. They sell a commodity, literally. Coffee is traded on the commodity markets...and we think we're in a "commoditized business!"

Yet, Starbucks commands 300% higher prices (or more) than the market rate for a cup of coffee. I'm a fan of their coffee, but it isn't the coffee that's getting them the premium. It's the process of buying the coffee that we pay so much for. The music playing overhead, the way you order, the fancy names of the coffee sizes, the comfy chairs.

It's all part of the buying process...and it's referable. It's worth talking about to your friends. And, it was especially unique and noteworthy as Starbucks was growing (before there was one every 30 paces in every city).

That's creating a referable sales process on a grand scale. But you don't have to create it on such a huge scale.

Case Study: A Surprisingly Simple Way To Make Your Process Referable

You can do, like one of my clients, Target Copy (targetcopy.com), did and do something small, but unexpected.

Target Copy is a local printing company and mail house in Tallahassee, Florida. They're known for really fast turnaround and often get people coming in to pickup rush orders.

UnstoppableCEO.net

When you place a rush order, they tell you what time you should come in to pick it up. And, occasionally, a customer will arrive before the order is ready or a production issue might delay completion of an order for a few minutes beyond the promised time.

Rather than simply make you stand around and wait, the folks at Target Copy innovated their "late delivery process."

Two doors down from Target Copy is a smoothie joint. The managers at Target Copy keep some gift cards for the smoothie place behind the front desk.

When a customer has to wait for an order that's taking a bit longer than expected, they get one of these cards and are invited to wait the additional few minutes in the comfort of the restaurant, enjoying a free smoothie, using the WiFi and, when their order is ready, they'll get a call or text message to come back.

That's innovating a process to make it referable. They don't have to use it often, but when they do, they turn a complaint into an experience the customer will talk about.

Imagine the conversation when Bob gets back to the office after being "inconvenienced" at Target Copy. He's going to say..."You won't believe what happened. I got there and the order was 15-minutes delayed, so they gave me this gift card for a free smoothie. I hung out at the smoothie place and got the strawberry crush with that protein

> powder...and a few minutes later they called me back to get my order. And did I mention I got a free smoothie! How cool is that!"

Process can be a powerful way to become more referable. But not every business can innovate their process. I work with a number of financial advisors selling life insurance and investments. The financial regulations they must comply with make it very difficult to innovate process.

If you can't innovate your product or your process there is ALWAYS one thing in your business that you can make more referable...

Your Personality

Innovate your personality? What? Is it even possible?

It is possible and it is the easiest, most attainable of the three places you can enhance your referability. Unlike product or service innovation, you don't need capital to develop a new or better product. And, unlike innovating your processes to become referable, you don't need to be particularly creative to develop lots of unique processes in your business that people will talk about.

It's also the most difficult for your competitors to copy. After all, they can't become YOU.

UnstoppableCEO.net

Becoming referable because of your personality is largely a formula. It's a formula that I'll explain in detail as we go through this book. And don't worry, if you think you don't have a personality, just follow the formula...it'll work for you, too!

Being referable because of your personality is ideal for professionals, small and medium companies in any industry and especially in businesses that require significant trust before a transaction happens. If you say that people buy from you because of "your relationship," then you already have a personality business and don't know it.

Becoming a referable personality doesn't mean that you'll change your real personality in any way. It simply means that you'll be the visible, human face of the business, and you'll do it in a way that allows you to open lots of doors with much less effort.

Case Study: How to Engineer a Referable Personality Even If You're in a Boring Business

My friend and client John Curry does this masterfully.

John is a retirement income expert. He works with people in their 40s through their 70s to help them have all the income they need for their lifetime. The financial products and services he sells are "commodities." There are several dozen people in his office who could sell a client the exact same product.

Clients hire John, not because his products are different or because they're delivered differently (he's in a highly regulated industry). No, they hire him because of WHO John is. And WHO he is in their eyes is no accident.

He has carefully crafted his "personality" to make him referable, to create familiarity and trust, and to be likable (to the right type of client).

John does this with a combination of authority and celebrity, both manufactured from scratch. To build his *authority* he became an *author*. Writing a short book--*Preparing for A Secure Retirement* (JohnHCurry.com/RetirementBook)--that forces prospects to see him differently...to see him and accept him as an author.

Later in this book you'll see a simple formula you can use to build your own book in no time flat.

But he doesn't stop there. John is a master at using the book as a prop to build his "celebrity persona." He's always got two things with him--a copy of his book, and a camera. At a conference he attended where George Foreman spoke (promoting his own new book), he took the opportunity to get a photo with Foreman. John held Foreman's book and Foreman held John's book. And he's done the same with other celebrities.

His clients and potential clients, who see these photos covering his office walls, associate John with "celebrity."

John uses the book, as a prop, to hold book signings, invite clients and their friends (referrals) to the book signing, creating more celebrity.

Beyond the book, John has now sponsored three concerts with a well known concert pianist who happens to be a client. John invites the community, partners with local charities who benefit from the proceeds of the concerts and plays MC during the event.

The events reinforce and enhance his celebrity personality. It is highly referable and attractive to John's ideal clients and prospects.

CHAPTER 2

Do I Trust You?

The New Referral Economy

We're in a new time in our evolution as a buying society and it's important for you to understand the shift that has happened (note, I didn't say "is happening" or is about to happen...it's already here). If you live in the First World, you have around you an abundance of choice. In fact, in most any category that you'd like to spend money you have essentially infinite choices.

What sounded like a good thing...more choice...actually makes our lives more difficult. More stressful. More uncertain. We've now got more options than we can possibly process and research. Many of which we know are "out there" but WE don't know of them. These "phantom" options induce even more stress.

We think, "What if I miss the thing that would be perfect for me?"

Along with the explosion of choice we now have, whether buying spark plugs or legal services, we've also been burned. In the United States we started down the path of dis-trust with Watergate. Our highest, most esteemed position was now untrustworthy.

And we thought, "What else can't be trusted around here?"

Then big business proved in certain cases to be unworthy of trust (think Enron). Then the church and church leaders. School teachers and scout leaders...the list is long, we are human after all.

The point of all of this is that to be successful in anything, including marketing and selling, you've got to start with an accurate assessment of the conditions you face. And selling today means you're selling to an untrusting consumer, facing an overwhelming, confusing array of choices.

As a result, buyers do two things: #1 They simply freeze up. Make no decision and live with whatever pain or problem they have until it becomes unbearable (or kills them). OR #2 They seek counsel and guidance from people they know and trust and even then, proceed cautiously.

Group #2 is important...they are the buyers. And they're looking for three things when they seek recommendations from the people in their social sphere.

1. They are trying to reduce their risk, or at least the risk they perceive to exist.

2. They want to abdicate some of their due diligence burden trusting that the person making the recommendation has done it already.

3. They help the prospect make a choice when facing an overwhelming number of options.

As I write this, my wife and I are in the process of building a home. Here's how we irrationally chose our builder...

We met the builder and his wife during the Parade of Homes. They were showing a home they'd just finished. And, it turned out my wife lived down the street from the builder's wife as a kid. They weren't close friends, but the familiarity added a small bit of trust. Then a few months passed and my wife discovered that this builder just finished a home for a vendor she's known for years at work. And this guy was really happy with the experience. More familiarity...more trust. Several months later, I learn that another business owner in my office building is building a new home. And he's using "our" builder...and has nothing but great things to say.

Two months later we're ready to start our home. Arguably the largest purchase we'll ever make together and likely the largest, most complex project we'll ever undertake as a couple. And we hire a company, without an interview, without competitive bids, without any competition at all.

We have four college degrees between the two of us and I've run two companies. So why would two seemingly intelligent and experienced people make such a big decision on what, as I write this, is clearly very little factual information?

Despite our education, neither of us is qualified to judge the quality of a contractor's work. Unless it looks obviously poor, we have no way to really know who's good and who's not...and we know it. And that unknowing caused significant stress before we chose this builder.

We know, through news reports and through real experiences within our networks, of people who have built homes and had builders abandon the work and take the money, leaving an empty bank account and an unfinished home. We know that Chinese dry-wall and a contractor-gone-bust make for a long, expensive life in an unsafe home. We know that, even barring those catastrophes, contractors do little things that tell us "they can't be trusted." (If you're a contractor, don't be offended, take note...this is how your buyers are thinking.)

Add it all up and there's a huge risk even embarking on building a home. In fact, for months my wife thought that we'd be better off simply buying an existing home (in other words, "It's too risky so let's avoid it all together").

But the familiarity and the good experiences of real people we know (and we don't know them well) give us comfort. Frankly, it allows us to abdicate responsibility for due diligence. (To date, I haven't checked with the State or the building department to find out if our builder has any complaints...I "should" do that!)

And that thin thread of trust turned this builder into "our builder." While all the rest are simply strangers.

We are sophisticated buyers who just made the largest purchase we'll ever make in the most illogical, unsophisticated way you can imagine. And we're not alone.

I don't care if you sell tires or trust funds or heart transplants...your buyers are doing the same silly exercise.

Why Referrals Are Vital

I hope you now see precisely why referrals are so vital today. When you had three brands to choose from, life was easy. Now, with an untrusting marketplace facing infinite choice, nobody moves without a recommendation. We want someone else to do the sifting and sorting of all the options so we don't have to...it's just too much work!

And the higher up you go in income and the more significant the purchase, the more your buyer will rely on recommendations.

They know that they're making a significant purchase decision and, for the most part, all the options could meet their needs. So the real question in everyone's mind is **"Who can I trust to keep their promises?"**

UnstoppableCEO.net

And, in my case, if two people I know trust my builder, have given him money and seem happy about it, then it is reasonable for me to think that when I give him money, I'll be happy about the result, too.

They trust him and I know them. Important...I didn't say I trusted them...I don't know either of the people who recommended this builder well enough to ever consider giving them the same sum of money. But I know them. And, lacking any other information, and needing some amount of trust to hang my decision on, it becomes enough.

That little bit of trust transferred to my wife and me. And that made the whole thing work.

A bit scary if you think about it.

The Seed Of Relationship

That little bit of trust is the seed of a relationship. Don't make the mistake of believing it is enough at the outset. Your job, once referral is received, is to engineer your business and your interactions with each new prospect to allow that seed to grow.

If you read the common advice on marketing and sales it all focuses on the tricks and tactics, the strategies and scripts to quickly turn prospect to customer. And if you're interested in a simple, sterile, transaction...an exchange of money for commodity widget or service, then put this book down and go read those. The tricks they teach may be sufficient for you.

In selling complex, high-ticket, big-decision products and services, that short term, tactical approach actually works against you. It erodes trust, rather than building it. And trust is essential to selling in this environment. Growing the significant level of trust required takes something most businesses underestimate...time.

Referral Resource

The best way to build trust quickly is to cultivate your own media platform (more on how that's done in Part 5). You can see a media platform in action by subscribing to *The Unstoppable CEO™ Online* (UnstoppableCEO.net/online) - my daily "media platform."

You'll get a first hand look at a simple way to build trust. You'll also get the latest updates on effective referral marketing.

A new referral comes with some trust, but they are still skeptical. The referral itself simply opens the door. It gets them to trust you just a little bit more than anyone else they could turn to, so they turn to you.

In my home building experience, the piece I left out is that once we arrived on the builder's radar, his wife, who is really the relationship builder, used the months between first contact and serious buying discussion to allow us to become familiar with them by inviting us to several family events in the neighborhood we're building in and to see homes similar to what we wanted in various stages of construction. To be honest, this was a minimal effort on their part. Much more could, and should be done to ensure that the accrual of trust is the result of system rather than happenstance. This book will show you how to operate at this higher level. But their efforts did work.

Blind Dates

How many blind dates end the evening as husband and wife? I imagine not many, at least outside of Las Vegas. My wife and I were married 358 days after we met and most considered it speedy. Why? Because in time you learn much about the character of a person...and a business. Yet, most businesses want you to go from blind introduction to consummated transaction in one step. (If only it were that easy, college would have been more fun!)

My own experience shows that the best clients mature over time. That introduction leads to education, then to familiarity and finally, trust. Then and only then is the prospect prepared to become an IDEAL client. This is an important point.

This is the secret to eliminating all competition. To becoming a category unto yourself.

Most car salesmen do the run to the altar. They "date" you out on the lot, but as quick as they can, they want you at the altar, in front of the sales manager to seal the deal. By contrast, Joe Girard the man who holds the Guinness Book of World Records title for World's Most Successful Salesman used time to his advantage. He built a system to capture the important dates in every one of his customers' lives. Birthdays, anniversaries, kids' and grandkids' birthdays. And he did a simple thing with each of those dates...he sent them a card, a note, he became a part of that celebration with them.

At the height of it all, he and two full-time assistants were required to keep up with the volume of cards to be sent. A lot of trouble for sure, considering he accomplished this between 1963 and 1978...before anyone knew what a Customer Relationship Management (CRM) system was.

Over the years he built such trust with his customers that they'd send everyone they knew to him. He sold cars by appointment only and new prospects were pre-sold before ever arriving.

In that 15-year period from '63 to '78 he sold 13,001 Chevrolets.

That's an average of 2.4 cars a day, 7 days a week, 365 days a year for 15 years.

And the guys and gals hanging around your local dealership hoping to get you to the altar the same day...who expect to go from "hello" to "will you marry me" in the first meeting...many are lucky if they average 2.4 sales a week (some...a month!).

By the time a prospect got to sit face to face with Joe Girard he'd engineered so much trust that he was simply facilitating buying...he was not *selling*.

What position would you rather be in?

How Long Are You Willing To Invest?

It's an important question. How long are you willing to invest in nurturing that little seed of trust and relationship before you attempt to harvest? Or before you give up and decide the seed will never bear fruit?

Financial advisor, John Curry, whom I introduced you to in Chapter 1, frequently tells stories of prospects calling his office, seemingly out of the blue, to make an appointment. When they arrive at his office, they're carrying a pile of postcards, newsletters and materials they've received from him. In one case, a prospect had a postcard from 7 years prior.

In another case, a couple arrived with a stack of his newsletters. And they left, having purchased a 6-figure annuity. They simply presented their financial symptoms to Curry, their financial doctor, who wrote a prescription to fix the problem.

Had he not diligently followed-up with, stayed-in-front-of, or become familiar to those prospects, it is unlikely he would have had the opportunity at all.

And if he did, it would have required significant "selling" to get the deal.

In Part 6, I'll show you how to construct such a follow-up system in just 90-minutes a month. The question you've got to answer is this, "Do I want a consistently increasing flow of pre-sold IDEAL clients calling me?"

I think I know the answer!

CHAPTER 3

Why You're Not Easy To Refer—And What To Do About It

The Most Overlooked Piece of The Puzzle

Most of us understand that we must do something referable and we must be trustworthy if referrals are to flow. You think, "If I do a good job, people will spread the word."

That puts the focus on your level of service. You certainly need to deliver on what's promised...and a little bit more. Yet, that's not the real key to unlocking 10-times more referrals.

No, in fact, it's nothing more than the entry fee to the dance. The minimum you need, to be included in the referral game.

What's missing is *EASE*.

Is it *easy* to refer you? If not, I guarantee you're sitting on a mountain of potential referrals that you're not getting today, because you've not identified and removed the roadblocks keeping them from you.

Roadblock #1: People will avoid anything that makes them uncomfortable. Every traditional referral carries implied sales pressure. And most of your clients and referral partners aren't great sales people. They're deathly afraid of selling and see it as, at some level, evil--to be avoided. So they will avoid it...and you'll get no referrals.

Roadblock #2: People are busy with their own lives and businesses. *They've already got a full plate, and you want them to do your prospecting for you.* They're uncomfortable about it to begin with, and they certainly don't have the time...you've got to make it so ridiculously simple that they can't use time as an excuse.

Roadblock #3: Even if they're willing, they don't know who, among all of their friends, family, colleagues and coworkers they should refer to you. The most common referral question used in the world is, *"Do you know anybody that might need xyz?"* And the answer is inevitably, *"Not off the top of my head, let me think about it."* You get that answer because the person you asked has never met anybody named "Anybody." You're asking them to do the work of researching who they should refer to you, and they don't know where to begin.

If those things sound silly or trivial to you, they are. But they are the reality that you're facing every time you ask for a referral. Your job is to eliminate the roadblocks.

What it Means To Be Easy To Refer... It's Not What You Think

By easy, I don't mean that you've given 50 members of your networking group your cards to pass out. And it has nothing to do with how promptly you return calls from new referrals. Responsiveness is not the same as being easy to refer. You've got to remove every possible friction point in your referral process--both the visible and the invisible.

Don't Make Me Work!

Want more referrals? Stop making other people do YOUR work. Business development is your job, not your clients' and not your referral partners' job. They've got enough to do with their own jobs, businesses, families and hobbies. If you expect them to put meaningful work into helping you attract more clients you're fooling yourself.

You've got to do all of the work for them. Meaning, identifying who you want to be introduced to. How to make the introductions. Even handling all the mechanics

(I'll cover exactly how to do this in Chapter 10). Their busy lives are just part of the problem.

Most business people ask for referrals in the most vague way. They say, "Do you know anybody (or somebody) who could use my help?" The first problem with this question is that it fails to frame the specific person or type of person you're interested in. In other words, you saying, "I don't know who my target market really includes, so would you think about it, figure it out and then send those people my way when you find them?"

This happens because few have ever really taken the time to decide exactly who they want to target. They don't know who their IDEAL client is and who it is not. Or, they're so desperate for business that they fear being specific and potentially missing out on some peripheral opportunity.

Not only does this kill your referral volume, it's also a bad place to be in business...you're not "for" anyone. When you're "for" a specific group of people, it's much easier for your clients and referral partners to know who to refer to you. My client, Proctor McInnis (McInnis Builders), is a great example of this idea. He's a commercial builder. Rather than be all things to all people, he's focused on helping franchise owners build new stores and restaurants. He's reduced it to a science.

And for his clients and referral partners it's very easy to refer him. They know exactly who his IDEAL client is...it's a person who's starting a new franchise location.

That's specific. The thinking is partly done, simply because he stands "for" franchise owners.

Even if you overcome the first problem and you do the thinking and are very specific about who you want to be referred to, there's a second problem that few ever understand or fix: Your clients and partners don't know how to introduce you. Or, more accurately, they don't know how to introduce you without it feeling *salesy*. In Part 2, I'm going to show you how to simplify the making of the introduction using what I call a *Referral Kit*. When you apply this concept the right way, as you'll see, clients and referral partners will want to pass it on, because doing so makes them look good.

See Real-World Examples of Referral Kits...
plus checklists, assessments and tools to improve
your referral marketing...all free at

UnstoppableCEO.net/ReferralResources

Grow Referrals 10x

The fastest way to grow referrals 10x is to make it easier to refer. You want to be able to start lots of relationships with the right types of people (your IDEAL clients) as quickly and effortlessly as possible.

The key shift in thinking that takes you from the old game of getting referrals onesie-twosie is understanding what a referral really is, and what it is not. When thinking about referrals, most picture a pre-sold client delivered to them all wrapped up in a bow. They have immediate need. They've been told they should work with you and only you and it's all a done deal. Who wouldn't want that?

But that's just a small part of the opportunity you have for getting referral business. Here's why...

According to the late Chet Holmes, author of *The Ultimate Sales Machine*, in any given market on any day, only 2% or 3% of the potential clients are ready to buy. Six to seven percent are open to the idea of buying. But another 30% know they have a problem.

Right now, your referral partners are waiting until someone is in such great need that they know with absolute certainty they should make the connection. And they're missing many of the people who are in their sphere of influence, and have the need and are ready to do something about it today.

If you're following the old referral model you're waiting too long to get introduced. And it's most often happening for you right at the point of the transaction. Better to open lots of doors with people who look like IDEAL clients, long before they're ready to buy.

You're then afforded the time necessary to educate that future IDEAL client on the problem they have and on YOU as they perfect solution. You have time to build trust in advance of the transaction and take it from mere transaction to relationship before money ever changes hands.

I'll show you exactly how to do that as we continue through this book together. I'll show you how to change the referral dynamic so that every time a referral partner refers you, they feel like they're promoting themselves (we'll cover a super effective way to do this in Part 3).

By the end of this book, you'll see how to orchestrate a system for attracting referrals that not only makes it easy for clients and referral partners to send business your way, it makes it so beneficial for them that they'll willingly and frequently open new doors for you.

You'll discover how to recruit a legion of "promoters" who will tell everyone they know about you. And you'll see how, in just 90-minutes per month, to become the most valuable resource your referral partners have and at the same time, follow-up with prospects like no-one-else...until they move from referral to client.

In the next section we're going to shift and get very practical. I'm going to share with you a tool that will form the foundation of your new *engineered* referral process. I call it a *Referral Kit*. And I'll share with you the exact components it must include to have the biggest impact.

Let's get to it!

Part Two:
How To Build Your
Referral Kit

CHAPTER 4

The Key To Making Referrals Easy

A *Referral Kit* is a widget, a thing, a prop that a client or referral partner can use to introduce you to a potential client. It usually consists of information that will affect the potential client four ways:

1. It helps them frame the problem and understand the consequences of inaction.

2. It helps them make sense of possible solutions.

3. It suggests a first step to resolve the prospect's problem (often a meeting with you).

4. It elevates, by design, your authority in the mind of the prospect to enhance trust.

Rather than simply introducing you, the person making the referral gives your referral kit to the prospective client. The job of the referral kit is designed to set the stage for a later, deeper, sales conversation...usually a 1-on-1 conversation.

Referral Kit Advantage #1
No Sales Pressure

In Chapter 1, we discussed the existence of implied sales pressure in every traditional referral. Using a referral kit, you eliminate that sales pressure by removing the immediate possibility of a sales meeting. The kit acts as a buffer between you and (your scary self) and the prospect.

Removing the sales pressure is extremely important. It facilitates easier referrals, because your clients and referral partners won't feel the awkwardness that prevents most from referring you. Especially in traditionally hard to refer businesses that deal with private, personal matters.

Your referral kit must appear free of "sales" clues. This is not simply your brochure. The purpose of a brochure is to sell. The purpose of your referral kit is to educate.

If you're the one educating a prospect on a problem they face...the one helping them better understand it...helping them see and analyze all of their options...and showing them the next step towards a solution, when they're ready, how do you think that's perceived?

You move from sales person to trusted advisor.

Referral Kit Advantage #2 - It's a Gift

Your referral kit, if done well, as I outline in the next two chapters, will be perceived by both the referrer and the referred prospect as a gift. Given by one, received by the other. Prospects who are facing a big problem will welcome an information "gift" in the form of a book, special report, CD or DVD if it helps them better understand the problem they face and the potential solutions.

Your referral kit puts you in the position of a giver. And, more importantly, it positions the person making the referral as a giver of the gift.

Think about that for a moment. Without a referral kit to give, the person who will refer you must essentially say, "You should really meet with my friend Sue so she can sell you some insurance." Do you want to meet Sue? I don't. And it really doesn't matter what smooth script you wrap around the introduction, because prospects hear it just like that.

But when you have a referral kit, it sounds more like this: "Bob, I just read this report that talked about your very problem, I think it will really help you. My friend Sue wrote it. Let me have her send you a copy."

Exchanging gifts is just more fun.

UnstoppableCEO.net

Referral Kit Advantage #3
It Positions You Above The Fray

Done right, your referral kit raises you to expert status. Now, if you're reading this and you're a member of one of the professions or you've got some alphabet soup of letters after your name, bestowed on you by a certifying authority, great! They, for the most part, are simply your ticket to the dance. They're not a differentiator in the eyes of a prospect.

If you're in a field that requires such credentials, then your competitors all have them too. So you're all "equally expert" to begin with. The playing field is level.

And, even if you've gone on to get advanced certifications, they are often meaningless to anyone outside your field. Remember, most aren't qualified to judge your qualifications (and they know it). So they look for other common signs of authority and expert status.

From the age of 3 or 4, through our early 20s we're taught to respect and learn from two types of people...those who publish (in virtually any format) and those who speak at the front of a room.

Your referral kit will put you in one, and possibly both, categories.

Rather than scream sales, your referral kit speaks to the wants and needs, the problems and opportunities of your IDEAL clients. While everyone else is shouting at the prospect to buy, you're calmly counseling them to make an informed choice.

Finally, your referral kit contains you...your (or your business') unique personality. That is an underused and potent advantage...and the easiest way to be perceived apart from all competition.

Referral Kit Advantage #4
It's Easy To Pass Along

Your referral kit has an advantage over you. It's a thing. An inanimate object. It's portable and non-threatening. It can be passed along without you. It is you and your business in a "box." This is an important point, don't overlook it.

Most business people are not easy to refer for all the reasons we've discussed. With your referral kit, you show up differently. To refer you, there's no need for all the back and forth to set appointments (friction), there's no scary sales pressure (friction) and the referrer doesn't have to worry about what to say (friction). In the past, I actually created a 1-page description of people I wanted to be referred to. At the bottom I had to write a script that people could use to explain what I did.

Imagine the difficulty in getting someone who's likely uncomfortable to begin with, to stumble through a script, try to put it in their own words, and make you sound like someone worth meeting.

UnstoppableCEO.net

The referral kit eliminates all of the friction because you're "packaged" in a way that carries lower commitment and cost than the traditional 1-to-1 referral. It is now easy for your referral partners and clients to spread the word about you far and wide...to many more (often all) of their contacts. You move from 1-to-1 referrals to 1-to-many. It is a leverage point for growth.

Referral Kit Advantage #5 - It Adds Value

Your referral kit is an educational tool. It should include information of real value to prospects. Insights that help them understand the significance of the problems they face and shine a light on a possible solution (hiring you or buying your product).

It is a "stealth" selling tool, and that's important. At this stage, the referral kit is NOT designed to make the sale. Instead, its sole purpose is to set the stage for the sale by positioning you and your business as a knowledgeable leader and expert. Your referral kit must give the IDEAL prospect something they didn't have before, some information or insight that helps them see more clearly.

If it does, it will be perceived as valuable and useful information, instead of a sales brochure. Brochures get thrown out. Important pieces of information, especially packaged as books, reports or audio CDs, get put on shelves after they are read...they stick around.

When you begin a relationship in sales mode you erode trust...you're there to take and prospects know it. When you begin a relationship by giving something of value, with no expectation, it increases trust. It puts you on the side of the prospect, rather than at odds with them.

CHAPTER 5

What Goes In Your Referral Kit

A great referral kit includes five parts. Each part is essential to building trust and positioning you and your business as leader, authority and expert. These are five building blocks that support one another. Omit one, and the structure is much weaker. Here are the five:

#1 Problems-Results-Questions

In creating the content for your kit you'll want to follow the old, proven advertising formula:

Present the problem...

Agitate the problem...

Solve the problem...

We begin by explaining the problem(s) your prospects face. They know they have the problem, even if they don't want to admit it. By stating it, we simply allow ourselves to get in sync with their thinking. To walk beside them. To show that we understand and empathize with their situation.

If you're good at 1-to-1 selling you know the power of this process. It allows you to bond with the prospect. And the best salespeople do it sincerely, out of true caring and desire to help another human.

This is a decidedly different approach than most of the brochures you'll ever see. They begin and end talking about themselves. They are like that guy at the party, that you just can't get away from. The one that you and your spouse have devised a rescue signal to escape, should you be cornered.

Start by asking yourself, "What problems do my prospects have...that they actually want solved?"

Notice the two part question. The second part is important. **"That they actually want solved."** All too often I see business people (usually someone who holds certifications) get all excited about a big problem their prospects face...but have absolutely no interest in solving.

Next, ask yourself, "What results do I create for clients that they can't create for themselves?" In the end, they don't want your product or service, they want the result. The old sales story goes, "There are millions of drill bits sold in America each year and not one person who bought a drill bit wanted a drill bit...they wanted the hole." Yes, it's a bit worn out, but it's very true. Speak to the results your prospects want, but can't get on their own, and you'll be speaking their language.

Then, list the questions that prospects and clients commonly ask. Theses questions are floating around in their heads right now, unanswered. Some will never ask them, but when you address them proactively, you immediately increase their trust in you.

Now take it a step further and list the questions that prospects *should* ask you before they buy a solution like yours. If they knew what you know, what questions would be important? This takes them beyond what's in their mind and shows them that you have deeper knowledge than they possess. It shows them that they'll benefit by listening to you.

#2 The First Step of The Solution

Once you've presented the problem your prospects face and you've talked about the consequences of the problem, should they let it fester, it's time to give them some relief. Let them take a peek at the solution...or at least the first step of the solution.

You need not, and should not, reveal the entire solution. At early stages of the buying process, it is unnecessary to reveal the full solution. More valuable, at that point, is understanding the full scope and consequences of the problem.

Take your prospect from where they are (staring a big problem in the face) to the future, when the problem is solved and life is grand. What does that future look like? Paint a vivid picture.

Then show them the very first step they should take to get that better future. By revealing a bit of the answer you are demonstrating transparency. **Transparency builds trust.**

#3 How To Go Deeper

Now that you've expressed your understanding of their problem and presented the start of the path to resolution, it's time to show them how to go deeper. To get all the help they need. To get the full solution to the problem. In other words, to buy.

I recommend to my clients that they create a low-barrier next step for new prospects. For a real estate agent it might be a "How to Sell Your Home Fast Audit"...a free 45-minute review of your home complete with recommendations for pricing, improvement and enhanced curb appeal, and at the end, an opportunity to list your home for sale with that real estate agent.

For a product company, it might be a demo of the product. For a custom product company, a design session geared towards helping the prospect visualize what their custom product will look like.

For most businesses selling complex things, in a long-sales cycle, at high prices, the next step is a 1-to-1 meeting of some kind. Essentially a sales meeting, but don't call it that. It's really an opportunity for the prospect to learn more about the solution to their problem or the result they want to achieve. And at the end, have the opportunity to make a decision...to solve the problem (buy) or not.

Notice in the real estate example, I didn't call it a "listing appointment." That's real estate lingo for a sales meeting...and prospects know it. Instead it is renamed to reflect the result the prospect wants and to indicate that there will be an analysis of their home. In other industries, especially professional services, the equivalent is the "free consultation." Now so commonly used, that the term has no meaning to prospects. And "free" is no benefit, because most every firm (in certain industries) offers the same free opportunity.

As you craft your next step offer, remember, you are scary to your prospects...they know you might sell them something. Understand this and account for it. Remove everything from the offer that makes it look like selling. Take away as much risk as possible, real *and* perceived.

#4 Prove It

Your skeptical prospect is looking for clues that you can be trusted, that you are real and that you (or your product) will do what you claim. Certainly you can say things to reassure, but far more powerful to have other people speak for you.

Enter the testimonial.

I'm shocked at how few business actually collect and use testimonials from happy clients. It is one of the best trust building tools available to you, and it's free. If you've got them, great. I'll show you how to use them in your referral kit. If you don't have any (or many) I'll show you a four-part formula for getting great testimonials in a moment.

Your prospects are looking for people like them. People who faced the problem they are facing and solved it by doing business with you. And they don't just want to hear how great you are, as most testimonials will tell them. No, they are seeking understanding..."did this person have my set of circumstances, did they share my fears and beliefs, was the problem they faced as severe as what I face...what did they do...how well did it work?"

Address these things and you have a powerful testimonial. And it will do far more "selling," far more effectively, than you ever could.

Now, here's my 4-part formula for a great testimonial. At this point I don't remember who I picked this technique up from...possibly my friend and marketing expert Dov Gordon...but with foggy memory, what the heck, I'll take credit!

This formula works best in an interview style, where you're asking a happy client these questions on the phone or on video. In either case, record the conversation. This interactive approach yields far better results than simply asking for a written reply, because you get the opportunity to ask the client to clarify or elaborate when needed.

#1 - Ask the prospect to introduce themselves and have them share anything important about who they are. For example, if you're trying to attract CEOs of large medical practices and you're interviewing a CEO of a large medical practice, make sure she says so.

#2 - Ask them to explain the challenge they faced. What was life like when that problem loomed over them? Did they search long and hard for a solution?

#3 - Have them describe the solution they found...you! How did they get relief?

#4 - What is life like now? Now that the problem is solved or the result delivered, how is life different, better than before?

Take your recorded interview and have it transcribed, then edit it into a polished testimonial using the best pieces of what the client shared. Send it to them and have them sign-off. You'll get fantastic testimonials using this method and by making it as easy as a 5-10 minute phone call, you'll find many more clients willing to do it for you.

> Get my simple, 4-part testimonial formula
> UnstoppableCEO.net/ReferralResources

UnstoppableCEO.net

#5 Don't Worry About Giving Away Too Much

The biggest objections I get when proposing to "give away" information to prospects about how to solve their problem is that by giving it all away, you'll somehow kill the sale...they won't need you anymore.

Not true. Your openness builds trust, and trust is essential before any transaction will take place.

And your IDEAL clients don't want a DIY solution. They want someone to take care of it for them. Those clients are the ones who will pay a premium price for the convenience and peace of mind of having you, the expert, do it for them. Laying out problem and solution in detail in your referral kit clearly demonstrates your knowledge and expertise.

And for service businesses, where product demonstration is often impossible (the surgeon can't give you a demo of the operation) it allows you to use the immense power of demonstration of ability, that the product sales guys have known and used for years.

See Real-World Examples of Referral Kits...
plus checklists, assessments and tools to improve
your referral marketing...all free at

UnstoppableCEO.net/ReferralResources

CHAPTER 6

The Best Format For Your Referral Kit

Now that you know how a referral kit will help you, and the five critical things your referral kit should communicate to your prospects, it's time to produce it. What you need to know is that the options for how to create your referral kit are good, better, best options...they all work. Effectiveness of format is dependent largely on two things:

1: How easy is it for people in YOUR market to share it?

2: Does the media/format you use enhance your prospect's perception of you as an authority?

Online or Offline?

Invariably, the very first question I get when working with a client to create their referral kit is, "Should we create something online?"

Usually, although they don't always say this, they want to steer things online (often to a document they can email) because they are CHEAP! Certainly online can work. The very first referral kit I created for my own business was online only...for about 30-days. (You can see it for yourself at UnstoppableCEO.net/ReferralResources.)

It quickly became clear that the opportunities for significant impact on the mind of a prospect came when I gave them something in the real world.

This may seem like a trivial difference to you. It is not.

Much higher value is placed on information that is published offline. After all, online information is FREE (i.e. has little value) and plentiful (i.e. commodity).

By contrast, we typically pay for access to offline information sources. To get the newspaper in physical form you pay. To get a book, you pay. To watch most TV, you pay. And recently, to access premium radio from the satellite radio companies, you pay.

Offline you pay.

Online is free.

Even though you will give away (in most cases) your referral kit, there is advantage in aligning with media formats that people already place monetary value on.

A second, more important reason to go offline is that offline pieces are visible. As I write this I've probably got over 1000 e-books and other pieces of referral kit material from all kinds of companies. Things I've downloaded over the years. They are "somewhere," trapped in the bowels of my hard drive.

Invisible to me.

Yet, just five feet to my left is a book shelf full of books from a mentor of mine (his referral kit). They are physical, visible to me and in his case, because he packaged his "kit" into book form, I'll likely never throw them away. In fact, it's almost taboo in our society to destroy books.

Point is...he's always with me in my office and has been for a number of years since I first met him through one of his "referral books," given to me by a friend.

There are thousands of other people who could do for me what he has done and is doing, yet he gets my money (well over $20,000 at this point) and has for close to a decade...'cause he's right there on my shelf...where I'm forced to be reminded of him every day. Not invisible, lost in a sea of emails and downloads soon forgotten.

The Special Report

The simplest of all formats is what I call the Special Report. The Special Report "kit" typically has three or more separate pieces that work together to position you and your business as an expert, educate the prospect on their problem and on you as the solution, and give them an easy next step towards buying.

The positioning and education is done in the first piece, a Special Report or White Paper. Proof and credibility are conveyed through the second piece—testimonials both inserted into the report and listed on a separate testimonial card. And the third piece is typically an offer page explaining what the prospect should do next to solve their problem (usually meeting 1-on-1 with you or one of your sales people) and giving them incentive to take that step.

The Special Report format is where most people start because it's easy to put together and can be done in a weekend. All you need is a word processor.

One word of caution. Don't be tempted to try and make your report "pretty." It does not need to appear as a glossy, polished marketing piece. In fact, that look will work against you because it screams, "I'm here to sell you something!" Instead, a simple, professional layout will work just fine. You want your report to appear as valuable information, not advertising.

The Audio CD

One of my personal favorite formats is the Audio CD. It is the easiest of all formats to create. You simply outline what you want to communicate to prospects, create questions following your outline and have someone interview you. The whole thing can be done in 90-minutes.

Audio has a number of advantages:

1. It's easy to consume. Important if your audience includes busy executives or professionals. Often the only down time they have is in the car going to and from work or to and from meetings. You can capture this lost time by sending them a CD they can listen to in the car.

2. CD's are cheap to produce and mail. At the time of this writing, to duplicate a CD, including a label, sleeve, cover letter, envelope and postage is less than $2. In return, **you get the opportunity to speak directly to your prospect for 30-60 minutes.** Good trade in my book.

3. Easy to create. As noted, you need an outline, some questions and an interviewer. The interviewer can be anyone. If you're physically in the same place you can use the voice recording function on most smartphones to record the interview. Small digital recorders work well too, and are available for less than $100. If you're not in the same place, you can use a service such as InstantTeleseminar.com or FreeConferenceCall.com to do the interview by phone. In this case, both parties call into

a number given to you by the service. Once on the line, you can record the call, then download an MP3 file of the call.

The Referral Book

Of all the possible formats for your referral kit, books are the best...the most effective. Let me explain why.

We have been trained from early in life to seek knowledge in books. Book authors are raised up as experts in their field. After all, "she wrote the book on _____."

Books are portable and easy to pass around. They carry a known value (most books sell for between $10 and $50). And they are sticky...most people don't throw away books.

Of all the ways you can wrap yourself in the clothes of the expert, the book is the highest and best available.

And the perception is that a book is difficult to write. For that reason, you're both respected as an author for simply completing the task that most fear and mostly immune to direct competition. Your competitors will never write a book, fearing the difficulty of the task.

Yet, writing a book need not be difficult. The audio recording used to make a CD could be transcribed and edited to make a book. And, in just 90-minutes of your time, you could have a 60-90 page book.

Or, you can do as I do. I write for an hour a day, from 5am-6am, 7 days a week. In an hour I write about 1,000 words (and I can't type fast). In a month that's 30,000 words. In 2-months, 60,000 words. Either way, you've got a book. Very small sacrifice.

Just imagine ending your next client meeting saying, "Bob, I just finished my book. I'd like you to have a copy. And I'd like to send a copy to 5 of your friends as a gift. Who should I send them to?"

One of my mentors is Dan Kennedy. I was introduced to Dan by a friend. We were having lunch and talking business and I asked about his recent success. And he said I needed to read this guy Kennedy. I left lunch and went to the bookstore on the way back to the office. Bought the book he recommended and read it.

In the book was a free offer to take a next step with Kennedy...to get two free issues of his newsletter. I did. Nearly 10 years later, I've faithfully paid him $60 a month. Plus $10,000 to be in a mastermind group and at least another $10,000 to attend conferences and events Kennedy hosts.

All because I was told to buy (yes, I had to spend money) a book...that's the value of the referral book. That's the value of being "the guy that wrote the book on _____."

Kennedy credits his books as the origin point for 80% of his newsletter subscribers and virtually all of his 5 and 6-figure consulting clients.

UnstoppableCEO.net

Now, here are your options for creating a book:

1. Write it yourself. As noted above, it can be completed in 30-60 days by writing for just an hour a day.

2. Record a 1-2 hour audio interview, have it transcribed and edited...book done!

3. Hire a ghostwriter.

4. Take all the articles you've written in the past and edit them together into book form.

There are any number of ways to get your book done. It does not need to be hard or painful. If the thought of writing a book is intimidating, start with an audio interview, put it on CD, then have it transcribed. Or, write one special report. Then write another. String together four or five reports into a book.

The advantages the book format gives you in positioning and "hand-around-ability" are worth the extra investment of time and energy. And both of the other formats I've described are great stepping stones to a full book. My first few referral kits were combined, improved and expanded upon to create this book. You can see my original referral kit at Unstoppable-CEO.net/ReferralResources

---

Information vs. Free Samples

We've focused on using information-based referral kits, but there is another option for some businesses-- free samples. I don't recommend this approach for service businesses as it usually devalues the service you're trying to sell. Samples tend to work less well as the complexity of the sales process increases.

Samples work well when you have such an amazing experience that once a prospect gets a taste they want to talk about it. Google used the idea of free samples to exponentially grow their Gmail service. Users had to apply to be on a waiting list for the service when it launched. And each new user was given five "invitations" to share with friends, so they too could get on the list. It can work, but it's not practical for most businesses selling high-ticket items.

Information is different. Information is essentially free to distribute, highly valued and can be instrumental in advancing the sales process. Every business has information about what they do that would be beneficial to clients and prospects. Usually the only thing that holds a business owner back, when thinking about sharing information is fear of giving away too much or giving aid to the competition.

For the most part both fears are unwarranted.

You can't give away too much. The accountant fears that giving away too much information about how to do a tax return will cause clients to do their own. And he misses the point...his clients don't hire him for what he knows (although that's a small part), they hire him to do what they DON'T WANT TO *DO*. You don't want the Do-It-Yourself client, you want the person who values his own time and energy so much that he views the service you provide or the product you sell as a bargain when compared to the time and effort he would need to expend to do it himself.

As for the fear of competitors, I've worked with businesses in 30 different industries and only one had such a proprietary process that they had legitimate concerns about sharing all the details. Most business owners think they have hidden advantages that must be kept secret. When in truth, the bigger opportunity is in attracting more of the market by sharing those advantages. In most cases, competitors will see it, acknowledge it as advantage, but will never act to do anything about it.

Don't waste time worrying about it and go get referred. In Part 3, I'll show you how.

Part Three:
Getting Referred

CHAPTER 7

Who Do You Want To Be Referred To?

Who Is Your Ideal Client?

When I'm working 1-on-1 with a client, usually the first obstacle we have to tackle is getting clear about what type of client they want to attract. I call this your IDEAL client. Most businesses have two, and only two, criteria for new clients--a heartbeat and a wallet.

And their marketing, networking and referral approach reflect this lack of clarity.

The problem with the approach is that prospects don't pay attention to messages that aren't "for them." And broad messages aimed at everyone meeting our two criteria are general and vague. They're not for ANY prospect, they are for ALL prospects. When you speak to everyone, you speak to no one.

The good news is that the problem is easy to fix. Simply choose who your IDEAL client is. The bad news...you have to choose.

That's the stumbling block for most businesses. And, to be truthful, it is what holds the majority of small businesses back. They never choose, so they operate without focus, and focus is necessary for rapid progress. I think I understand why it's difficult for business people to get this kind of laser focus...it's not that choosing is hard.

Talk to any business owner and they'll tell you who their best clients are and they'll tell you how great it would be if all of their clients were like their best clients. But they don't choose to focus either because they don't know they can, or more often, because they're afraid to say to the universe that there is some business they don't want.

Yet, real and rapid progress predictably comes when you focus on attracting your IDEAL client.

Yes, that means you must choose your IDEAL client (more on how to clarify that in a moment) and focus your marketing and referral energy towards attracting that type of client. It does not mean that you've got to turn away clients that want to pay you, but don't fit the profile. And it doesn't mean you're limited to that one type of IDEAL client forever.

What it does mean is that your client attraction is focused only on attracting IDEAL clients. If others come and you want to accommodate them, by all means do so. It also means that if you want to be effective, you target ONE type of client to begin with.

Over time you may add other types of IDEAL clients, for example an OB/GYN practice might target both women thinking of starting a family and women approaching menopause. As you might imagine, if you try to attract the menopausal women by talking about pregnancy you're in for tough sledding. Ditto if you reverse the two. And if you talk in your referral kit about women's health issues in general, you're not speaking to the specific problems, fears and dreams of either group.

Instead, pick one group to begin with and create a referral kit tailored to that group. Apply the system I'll show you in the next few chapters to that group. Get the flow of new referrals and clients working. Then go back and repeat the process for your next market.

You'll get results more quickly and you'll have a blueprint to build on as you add each new market.

How to Create A Picture Of Your IDEAL Client With These Four Questions

Now, write a narrative description of your IDEAL client. Use these four questions as your guide. Your description might be a couple of paragraphs or a couple of pages. The more detailed and deep your understanding of your IDEAL client the better.

1. What Do They Look Like?

Not literally their physical appearance, but in general, how do you know an IDEAL client when you see one? I recommend writing a short narrative paragraph that describes the general qualities of your IDEAL client. In our OB/GYN example, for the soon-to-be-pregnant group you might write:

"My IDEAL client is a young professional woman in her mid-20s to mid-30s. College educated, married, living in the northeast section of town. Her income is $70,000 or more, she is health conscious and exercises. She is covered by a premium employer health plan that allows her to choose her own doctor..."

And you could go on to describe every detail of your IDEAL client. I'm guessing you've probably never done an exercise like this...it will give you great clarity about who you want to do business with.

Be as specific as you can be in your description. Don't worry about being too choosy as you describe your IDEAL client...after all, this is the IDEAL. You can always take away some of your criteria to expand the market size. In our example above, we might relax the health plan or exercise criteria. The important thing to do is get everything on paper first, then edit if you need to.

2. Where Do They Hang Out?

Now that you've written a clear description of your IDEAL client make a list of the places they "hang out." Are they online or offline? On Facebook? At the Chamber of Commerce, Rotary, the industry conference? What magazines and websites do they read? What other businesses do they work with? What email lists are they on? What associations do they belong to?

You're looking for all the places and ways you can reach them. This list will help you identify potential referral partners, which we'll cover in the next chapter.

3. How Do They Think?

How do they think and make decisions? We know from studies that all buying comes from emotion. Either the emotion of fear or the emotion of desire. But we analyze options differently based on our natural thought styles. Some may agonize over every detail, spec and fact to justify their decision to buy to their very logical self. Others may simply need a big picture, gut feel for the decision. It's useful to understand how your IDEAL clients make the buying decision..and there's a good chance you'll have a mix of thinking styles.

In both cases you need to give them what they want to justify their buying decision.

UnstoppableCEO.net

4. Who Are Their Friends?

Who are the influencers in their lives? Socially, professionally? What companies do they already do business with and trust? Understanding who they associate with will help you build a strategy for reaching them through referral. The goal is to see the whole of their interactions with people. The opportunities lie in finding entry into their world in places that your competition fails to see.

Narrow Focus = Speed To Results + Leverage

It's worth mentioning again...as you work to identify your IDEAL client type, a narrow, niche focus is best. By focusing in, you direct all of your energy to attracting your IDEAL client and you'll find that results come easier and faster. Time and again, I've watched business owners stubbornly go after any and all business. They never really get momentum and they struggle to move from 1-on-1 sales where every client you attract is a custom job, to a place of leverage. Where you have a niche message finely tuned to the fears and desires of your specific IDEAL client.

CHAPTER 8

Stop Chasing "Referral Partners" and Start Cultivating "Promoters"

What Are Promoters?

You've undoubtedly got referral partners. Businesses that you're friendly with and with whom you exchange leads. That's great, but it's usually a one-at-a-time exercise.

To attract many more referrals, with less effort and without "asking" for the referral, we need a different approach. Instead of one-at-a-time, you need to build a system that makes it easy for you to get introduced to many-at-one-time.

To do that, we're going to elevate your referral partners to "Promoters." Promoters will, if it's easy for them and valuable for their relationships, promote you to many, often all of their contacts at once.

Armed with your referral kit and with the strategies I'll share with you in the next two chapters you'll move from getting a referral here or there, to getting dozens, even hundreds of introductions, "open doors" as I like to call them, at one time. I know that may seem too good to be true, but my clients and I have experienced it. To date, the record for new introductions using these methods is 458 in one week.

But you don't need that many to get fantastic business results. One client of mine can trace over $1,000,000 in new business in one year from referrals that got his referral kit through one of his promoters. And he averages 10-20 new referrals a week (yet most in his industry get one or two a month).

In the next section I'll take you step-by-step through the process of identifying and attracting a solid stable of Promoters.

Who Is Your IDEAL Client Already Listening To?

To begin building your list of Promoters, start with the people and businesses your IDEAL prospects are already doing business with or already listening to. This is not a new exercise. Nearly every book on referral marketing will tell you to look at complimentary businesses to build referral partnerships. We're going to do that here, then, we're going to approach them very differently, as I'll describe in the next chapter.

For now, I want you to make three lists. First list the people and businesses your IDEAL prospects buy from at work. And I want you to think about EVERYTHING they buy. Don't edit the list or make any judgements at this point. Just get it down on paper.

In my first business, we found that a great source of referrals was the copier salesman. His business was totally unrelated to ours, but he was in the office of every one of our IDEAL prospects. I want you to think broadly as you make this list to cover every vendor or type of business you can think of.

Next, make a list of the people and businesses your IDEAL prospects buy from at home. Where are they spending their money off-the-clock? Again, think broadly. Simply brainstorm now, don't edit the list yet.

Finally, make a list of the places you can reach your IDEAL client that your competition doesn't know about. Make your list by looking at the first two and looking at your IDEAL client profile. In both places there are clues to the media and organizations your clients pay attention to. Which ones do your competitors know about? Which ones are invisible to them?

For example, maybe your IDEAL prospects are all in a particular industry and participate in the industry association. You know and your competitors know it. You probably want to be there, but it's always more difficult with competition.

By contrast, there are probably other groups that contain some of your IDEAL prospects that are not related to that industry, yet you'll find prospects there. There are publications and websites and other media that your prospects read that is unrelated to the main business they're in. Make a list of these places. Again, just make the list. Don't edit.

Each of these lists gives you starting points for finding Promoters. Now let's look at the five criteria to use when evaluating a Promoter.

The 5 Essential Criteria for Choosing Promoters

There are five criteria I use when evaluating potential promoters. It's important to have criteria. It will keep you from working with the wrong promoters, and save many headaches!

Promoter Criteria #1: Are they friendly and open to working together?

If they're a jerk or not keen on working with you, in other words, if you have to do a lot of convincing, they will probably disappoint you as a Promoter. They won't be effective and likely won't be someone you want to introduce to your own audience of prospects and clients. If this is the case, just don't go there at all.

Promoter Criteria #2: Are they selling to the same pool of people you sell to?

Do they fit one of the three lists you created in the last section? If not, why waste your time?

Promoter Criteria #3: Do they have a list of prospects, partners and clients?

You don't need promoters with big lists (although big lists are great). You do need promoters with lists. Seems obvious, I know, but you'd be amazed at the number of business people you come across that don't have a list of prospects and customers.

Promoter Criteria #4: Do they have some expertise that YOUR clients and prospects might find interesting?

As you'll soon see, you want to find Promoters whom you would feel comfortable promoting to your own list of prospects and clients. If you're not comfortable doing so, then you'll end up with a one-way flow of value in your relationship and it won't work over the long-term.

Promoter Criteria #5: Are they people you like?

This is may be the most important. If you can't stand them, no matter how valuable they might be, it won't work. You're looking for strong, long-term relationships with people who have similar values and congruent experience. You've got to generally like them...not necessarily be best friends...but like them and what they stand for.

You'll find it much easier to evaluate potential Promoters if you run them past these five criteria.

> Download the Promoter Selection Checklist
> UnstoppableCEO.net/ReferralResources

WARNING: If you chase them, they'll run away

Now for a warning...

The usual approach I see business people use when trying to start a relationship with a referral partner is this: "Let's see how we can help each other."

When I hear this, most of the time the person saying it means, "Let's meet for coffee so I can find out who you know, then I'll ask you for introductions." It's a one-way street, and I'm going the wrong way.

This approach rarely leads to a beneficial relationship. In fact, it often scares people off because they've heard it before and they know that it's unlikely to lead to any productive business.

Instead, you must show up differently than every other professional out there who's chasing referral partners. If you chase them, they'll run away. Instead, give value first. Massive value.

Yes, you've probably heard that before. The idea that you give and you gain is not new. Yet, I find few business people know how to do it. The usual method is to try to find a referral for the potential referral partner, but this can take time. You need to build relationship and gain trust. Often it's done in a sort of forced way and it's rarely successful.

In the next chapter I'll show you how to deliver massive value to your Promoters. You'll deliver it quickly and in fact, it will be the easiest way for you to build relationships "up the ladder" that you've ever experienced. What is this method? Why does it work so well and so quickly?

You'll have to read on to find out!

CHAPTER 9

Turn Your Promoters Into Stars

The Johnny Carson Star Creation Method

Now that you've started to build your list of promoters it's time to make them "famous." Or at least feel like it...

Our goal is to give massive value to the people we'd like to have as our promoters. To build relationship with them rapidly. And to give them an opportunity to be the star in the spotlight.

There's no better example of how to instantly create stars than the legend of late night TV, Johnny Carson.

When Carson hosted the Tonight Show he could take you from unknown to a nationwide (even worldwide) sensation in one show. He arrived consistently, every evening, in your living room. He was personal. You got a true sense of who Johnny was...he was real. And because he was real, and he was there in the living room night-after-night he built tremendous trust with his audience.

Johnny was the taste maker for an entire country and beyond. If he recommended someone or something, you trusted his judgement. He became a filter for his audience, who trusted him to bring only the best new band or comedian or public figure to the living room for a chat.

Carson's power to influence his audience was immense.

We're going to use the same techniques that Johnny used to shine a bright light on your Promoters. To turn them into stars to your audience. And to make them <u>feel like</u> stars. To see you as a valuable gateway to your audience.

Now, don't worry. You don't need a big audience to begin with. In the next chapter I'll show you how to get your Promoters to promote you and you'll see your audience grow rapidly.

So what was the secret to Johnny's success?

It was really quite simple. He let us eavesdrop on his conversations with important people. We got to sit in and feel as if we were there. In the process we felt we knew Johnny intimately, and we felt we knew his guests.

The Power of The Interview

Carson used interviews with his guests to bring them to us in a way we could relate to. Likewise, you can build rapid relationships with your Promoters by interviewing them and sending that interview to your audience. You'll be the star maker for your audience and your Promoters will be the stars.

Your audience--your prospects, clients and other potential Promoters--will get to eavesdrop on your conversations. They'll get valuable information from the smart people you interview. And they'll walk away feeling like they know you, even if you've never met. And, importantly, both your audience and the Promoters you interview will see you as an authority. This is critical to attracting clients and building trust in advance of a sale.

The interview format is the key. To begin with, it's easy to implement. Unlike other marketing methods you don't have to learn a script, be a copywriter or a web expert. You simply need to have conversations. I'm guessing you already know how that works.

So let's get started...

Three Ways to do Your Interviews

Let's not make this any more complicated than it has to be. There are really just three ways to conduct your interviews. Here's the scoop on each one.

UnstoppableCEO.net

Text Based Interviews:

No technology required (well, maybe email). In a text based interview you simply develop a list of questions. Send them to your promoter. They answer them and send them back. It couldn't be more simple. You might use the same set of questions for each person, or you may do a little research and customize the questions to each promoter's expertise. My colleague, Jason Leister, does the text interview format masterfully with his *Five Questions* series. And he's landed some "big names" in his industry, despite the fact that Jason's not famous.

Video Based Interviews:

OK...a little more technology. Video interviews can work really well, too. Hey, Johnny Carson used them! You and your promoter can get on Skype or a Google Hangout, turn on your webcams and have a conversation. In fact, on Google Hangouts, people can watch live or watch a recording. The recording tool is built in and you can instantly post the interview to YouTube. Skype works well, too, but you'll need separate screen recording software to record the video, then post it to YouTube or some other place where your audience can access it.

Audio Based Interviews (My Personal Favorite):

Personally, I prefer audio. An audio interview allows your audience to hear your voice and hear the Promoter you are interviewing. Because they can hear your voice, you will build faster relationship with every person who listens...that's the power of the human voice. Video is the same in this regard, but I prefer audio. Here's why...

Audio is highly portable. It can be consumed when you're driving, working out, cleaning the house or mowing the lawn. It's hands AND eyes free. This opens up a huge number of opportunities for you to grab time with your audience when they're able to listen, but they couldn't read or watch a video.

It's cheap and easy to distribute an audio interview. It can be easily delivered online as a simple download or as a podcast. And it can be delivered offline (very powerful if you're trying to reach busy executives) by sending it on a CD for about $2 per person.

It's also very easy for the Promoters you want to interview. They may not have a web cam or be comfortable with that technology. They may not be great writers. But they sure can have a conversation on a telephone!

And that's all that's needed. Using a service such as FreeConferenceCall.com or InstantTeleseminar.com, you and your Promoter simply call in using a special phone number. You press a couple of buttons on your phone and the call is recorded. At the end of your interview, you login to the website for the service and download the recording (usually in MP3 format, ready for publication).

The whole thing can be done in a 20-30 minute phone call.

UnstoppableCEO.net

Why Interviews Work Like Crazy

Sounds so simple...interview the people you want to build Promoter relationships with, pull out their expertise and share it with your clients and prospects. You're probably wondering, why does this work?

It works on several levels...

First, it positions you very differently from the person who approaches a promoter saying, "Let's see how we can help each other get more business." Chances are the Promoters you approach for an interview have never been asked to give one before. They'll feel flattered...special.

When was the last time you felt flattered or special when asked to have one of those "let's work together" coffee dates?

Next, you're approaching them, not saying "Let's work together," but instead saying, "I think you're a real expert at what you do. You have valuable knowledge that my clients and prospects would benefit from. Would you be willing to share it with them? And, in the process, they'll all get to know who you are."

Not only are you making them feel good by stroking the ego (and there's absolutely nothing wrong with that), you're giving them a genuine opportunity to grow their own business. Just as all of the experts say, you're giving first...and you're giving massive value.

For your Promoters there is no downside. It's a no-brainer decision to say YES.

And, it's much easier for you to give like this than to scramble around to find a referral for someone you just met, in the hopes that it will put you in their good graces.

Look, the 1-by-1 referral model works. I've made it work. I've seen others make it work. But it takes tremendous effort for a long period of time to make it work effectively.

The method outlined in this chapter is simply easier. Results come much faster. And, it can open doors for you with promoters who are "up the ladder" from where you are, with people who are more successful and harder to reach (maybe even impossible to reach) using other methods.

Boost Your Own Status and Credibility With Zero Extra Effort

When I first present this concept to clients there is one piece they don't recognize at first, and it's important. By being the guy or gal doing the interviewing you gain tremendous advantage with your own prospects and clients.

Just as Johnny Carson did, you become the "taste maker" for your audience. The conduit through which they get access to the experts you interview. Yes, you're elevating your promoters and you're introducing them to your audience. And at the same time you're becoming the person that's uber connected with experts and influential people. You will become a celebrity to your audience.

Get Introduced to Your Promoter's Audience

In the next chapter, I'll share how to get your promoters to share you and your referral kit with their audience. But once you've interviewed them, you have a fantastic opportunity to get them to put you in front of their audience right away. And, they'll love to do it.

Simply suggest (and often they'll ask) that your promoter share your interview with his own prospects and clients. It could be as simple as emailing them a link to listen to the interview online (hosted on your website of course!). Or you could send them all an audio CD of the interview in the mail.

What ever method you use, what better way to "meet" your promoter's prospects and clients for the first time. You're being introduced to them as a celebrity and expert on the same level (or above) the person you interview.

Again, there's nothing but upside to them agreeing to send it...remember you're making them look like a star!

You've now aligned your goal (getting referred) with their own self-interest (being an expert to their audience of clients and prospects). It's very powerful and all three parties win...you, your promoter and their audience.

Discover The Secret Sauce

If there's a secret sauce to making this all work...for you and for your promoter, it's this: Your purpose in doing these interviews is to shine the spotlight on your promoters and turn them into stars. This may be their one and only opportunity to do something that approaches celebrity. Make it a special experience.

This is selfless promotion at its best. Yes you will benefit, but the benefits you get are simply natural byproducts of this process. This is all about THEM.

When you make it all about THEM, you actually gain immense power and prestige as the interviewer...the selector of experts...the maker of celebrities within this community.

You don't need to hog the spotlight during the interviews. Keep it on your promoter.

Don't be shy about telling everyone who listens to or reads your interview how to connect with your promoter if they want to learn more. And be sure to funnel any comments or feedback you get from your audience to your promoter (you'll get many kind and thankful words).

Remember, It's an Audition

Every interview you do is an audition...for you! It's an audition that your next promoters will see. This is your opportunity to show them how you'll handle them when they are interviewed.

They'll see that you send out the interview to your audience, because you'll send every interview to your future promoters, too! If you show them that being interviewed by you has huge value, they'll be chasing you trying to be interviewed.

No more begging for meetings, hoping that someone will, maybe, pass you a referral! What a better way to grow your business!

CHAPTER 10

How To Get Massively Referred

Now Get 'Em To Promote You

I hope you've started scheduling your interviews and, ideally, you've got one under your belt by now.

Your interviews will generate referrals...new people being introduced to your business, and by themselves, the interviews often lead to new business as the people you interview share it with their clients and contacts. Now we want to take it a step further...

You've built credibility and relationship with your endorsers. It's time to turn the tables and get them to promote you. Something you need to understand going into this...some of the people you interview will choose not to promote you to their list.

It's OK...it's just part of the game. But most will.

So how do you get someone to promote you? You ask! "But wait!" you say, "Isn't this process supposed to eliminate the need to ask for anything?"

No...you still have to ask for what you want. The difference is in what you're asking for and how it's perceived (valuable vs. slimy).

In the old model of getting referrals, it's focused on you extracting from the relationship to get a referral.

In the new model, even as you ask to be referred, you're leading with something valuable.

Enter your referral kit.

The referral kit is the key to opening up more referrals using this method.

It's different...most companies don't have anything like it. It's useful to people who experience the problems you can solve.

It shows that you're an expert who cares about helping people regardless of whether or not money changes hands. I'm not saying we're not trying to make money. Of course you must to stay in business, grow and have the things you want to have.

The difference is in *the purity of your intent.* If you're only out for the money, it shows.

That selfish intent erodes trust (you're not seen as an honest broker) and it repels people.

If, however, you lead with something valuable that comes with no strings...you're seen as giving and trustworthy. Relationship with your prospect builds more quickly because their defenses are down. And it's easier for them to take the next step towards a solution to their problem.

Three Ways To Get Promoted

#1 The Endorsed Mailing (Print Letter or Email)

One of the simplest and most effective ways to get promoted is the endorsed letter. In an endorsed letter, your promoter sends a letter (on his or her letterhead) or email to his or her list of clients/contacts offering your referral kit.

Here's a sample letter (download a template you can modify at UnstoppableCEO.net/ReferralResources).

May 1, 2013
Bob Jones
4321 First Street
Anytown, NJ 45678

Dear Bob,

I'm writing to introduce you to Jane Palmer. Jane is a colleague and someone you should know. She's in the commercial insurance business and is someone I trust.

Recently, Jane published a guide for business owners titled: "13 Policy Tweaks That Are Costing You Thousands." I read the guide and immediately found a couple of items I needed to address. And I imagine you'll find the same when you read it.

I asked Jane to make her guide available to any of my clients and friends that would like a copy and she agreed. Not only that, she agreed to cover the cost of printing and mailing it to you.

I encourage you to give Jane a quick call to let her know you'd like a copy. Her phone number is (850) 345-6789. You can also drop her an email at jane@smartinsurance.com.

Sincerely,

Mike Edwards
President

P.S. I think she only had 50 copies printed so I suggest you give her a call now, while it's fresh in your mind (and while she's still got copies available).

Here's how to ask an endorser to promote you:

"Hi Bob, I published this guide recently on 7 ways small business owners can cut their tax bill. It's a collection of some of the most common tax mistakes I see in my accounting practice every year. I know you have a number of small business clients, too. Do you think they would benefit from reading it?"

Bob says, *"Yes!"*

"Great. Here's what I propose we do...I think we should send them a letter/email offering the guide. It should probably come from you, but I'll be happy to write a draft for you to edit if that makes it easy for you. In the letter we can ask them to call my office to request a copy...or send me an email. That way we're not sending it to anyone who doesn't want it. How does that sound?"

Bob may have a couple of questions about getting it done. Such as...

"How will we handle the printing and mailing?" Answer: Offer to take care of everything if it makes Bob's life easier.

"What do you get out of it?" Answer: I'll get to meet some people who might one day need my services and you'll get to help your clients solve a big problem.

"Why not just send the full guide out to everyone?" Answer: Two reasons...First, printing and mailing the guide is a large expense compared to sending a letter...no sense in wasting money on those who don't want it. Second, I've always found that people prefer to have a choice about the information they receive.

Once you've got agreement, do the following:

1. Set a date for the mailing/email to go out.
2. If you're using a seminar or webinar as your referral kit, set a date/time for the event.
3. Use the appropriate planning worksheet to plan out the steps you'll need to follow to make the endorsement happen.
4. Follow the checklist and make it happen!

For a complete set of planning worksheets and checklists get the Unstoppable Referrals home study course at UnstoppableCEO.net/ReferralCourse.

#2 The Newsletter Method

The newsletter method is often easier than an endorsed mailing.

You don't have to handle the printing and mailing...just put together an article.

Usually the article will be short: 500-800 words.

Your promoter, who publishes the newsletter, will be able to tell you exactly how long your article should be. Your article does not need to solve the problem for the reader. It simply needs to give them an "ah-ha" moment. A moment of increased understanding.

Here's my favorite "formula" for writing these articles: P.A.S.

P = Problem: State the problem that your prospects (the readers) face.

A = Agitate the problem: Next, tell them why the problem is bad. Tell them what is likely to occur if the problem is left unsolved.

S = Solution: Now that you've framed the problem and the negative impact of ignoring it, offer a solution.

You don't need to explain the entire solution, simply state what the solution is.

Then, (and this is critical) at the bottom of your article you'll include an author's bio. But don't give biographical information...no-one really cares.

Instead say something like this:

Jane Palmer is the author of "13 Insurance Policy Tweaks That Are Costing You Thousands." To get a free copy of the report call 123-4567 or email report@janepalmer.com.

Unlike magazines, most newsletter publishers won't even think to ask if your article has been published elsewhere. So...you can reuse the same article again and again in different publications.

> See Sample Newsletters:
> UnstoppableCEO.net/ReferralResources

#3 Seminars and Webinars

Seminars, webinars and events can be very effective "referral kits." They are not a kit in the sense that you can hand it to someone. But rather, a different way to convey the information you compiled in your referral kit.

These types of events typically have the highest conversion rates of any of the referral methods we've covered. Why?

Because they allow you to have face-to-face interaction with your prospects. Trust is built much faster, thus you can move prospects to a higher level of commitment more quickly.

With all of that benefit also comes increased cost and added complexity. But if you're selling high-ticket products or services you should probably have a seminar, webinar or event in your referral arsenal. The approach is almost identical to an endorsed mailing.

You'll use essentially the same words to propose an event.

With an event you'll want to make sure to have a way for prospects to register. Registrations can be collected on your website, by email/fax or by phone.

One of the big hangups I hear from business people who use seminars and webinars to attract referrals has to do with the size of the audience.

Yes, we'd all like to be in front of 100, 500 or 1,000 prospects at each event. But the reality is that you'll probably see attendance range between 5 and 50...depending on what you're offering.

The key with this method is to do a seminar or webinar regularly (monthly). My private clients who have been most successful with this method will hold the event even if just one or two people show up (rare).

And what they've found is that almost every event leads to a new client. Some are seeing 70-90% of attendees booking a sales appointment at the event.

Don't let them leave the event without the opportunity for setting an appointment. If you try to get the appointments with a follow-up call, letter or email you will be disappointed with the results.

Stay In Control

All three of the methods I've described work. I've personally used every one to great success and my clients use them month-in and month-out.

Together we've learned that the key to getting promoters to do any one of those techniques for you is to do all the work yourself. To keep control.

Here's why...

Your Promoter is BUSY. This will not be the highest item on their priority list (don't even expect it to be). And, they've probably never done anything like it before. They won't know the steps like you do, so they'll bog down. If you rely on them to get it all organized you'll be frustrated.

The answer is simple. You offer to do all the work. I guarantee they'll take you up on it!

And there's good reason to do it yourself: this is your business' development strategy. It's your job to execute it anyway. If you want the fastest, easiest path to more referrals...more clients...then do the work yourself. 'Nuff said!

How To Capture The Referrals You Get

So you've lined up a promoter to send an endorsed letter or hold a joint event (or whatever first method you choose) and you can't wait for the referrals to come rolling in. There's just one more piece that you must have in place.

How will they respond and how will you capture their name and contact information?

You have several good options.

The first and most obvious is to have them call your office phone number. Start here if you must, but understand that it will likely reduce the number of people who contact you for your referral kit. Those that do call will be closer to the end of the buying cycle and their pain or problem will be more acute. The reason you'll get fewer is that people want to avoid talking to a salesperson-- which might occur if they must call your office and speak to a human. This also limits you to lead capture during business hours.

For many markets the web is the ideal place to capture leads. You'll want to have a special page on your website that re-sells them on the benefits of having your referral kit. And, on that page, have a form to take their contact information. You can connect the form to your CRM software or email marketing software to have the referral kit delivered instantly by email or you can have it notify someone on your staff to mail a hardcopy of the kit if you plan to send it offline. Both methods work, depending on the market and your goals.

How to Automate Your Referral Marketing and Save 10 Hours a Week

As you start to get dozens of referrals a week, following up and delivering your referral kit will become a time consuming chore.

The best solution is to automate your response when a new referral comes to you. If they request your kit on the web, you can automatically and instantly deliver it by email. And if you prefer to send something offline (as I do), you can arrange to have a fulfillment house handle the printing and mailing of your referral kits.

To make all of that happen you need software on the backend to take the requests and either email the right file or send a notification to the fulfillment house with the mailing address for each referral.

Thankfully, there are a number of good, inexpensive solutions for this function. My preferred tool is Infusionsoft. I've used it for close to a decade with very good results. You can check it out and see a demo at UnstoppableCEO.net/Infusionsoft.

In addition to a response page on your website, you can offer a fax order form that prospects complete and fax to your office. This works well in many industries where fax is still heavily used, such as banking, medicine and law.

The often overlooked, yet very effective means of lead capture is the free recorded message. A free recorded message is simply a special voicemail line. You record a message that, like the webpage, re-sells the prospect on the benefits of the referral kit. At the end of your message, you ask the prospect to leave their name and contact information so you can send them the referral kit. The key is to make it clear that they are calling a recorded message--they won't have to talk to a human. This is another great way to have around-the-clock lead capture.

For best results combine some or all of these methods.

Part Four:
How to Get Clients to Refer You Without The Awkward "Ask"

CHAPTER 11

The Reverse Prospecting
Secret

They say birds of a feather, flock together. Clients usually do, too. That's one of the reasons referrals work so well. Once you've won a few IDEAL clients, chances are they're hanging out with other IDEAL potential clients.

Yet, as we discussed in Chapter 1, getting them to refer you can be difficult--even if they like you and appreciate what your company does for them. Your referral kit, gives you the "prop" to make the referral easier. If you've done it well, it will be perceived as a useful gift.

Now the question is, "Who should they give it to?"

The easiest way to help them figure out who should get it is to do "Reverse Prospecting." Let me explain...

Reverse prospecting is simply reverse engineering your client's network of contacts, then presenting her with a list of people that you know she knows or, at least, is likely to know. To do this, you've got to know your clients well. You need to understand who they associate with--where they work, what industry associations they belong to, what social organizations they participate in, where they go to church and so on.

Not all of these examples will fit your prospects. You've got to determine, which groups bring your client in contact with other IDEAL prospects.

Then you get or compile a list of the people in the groups you've identified (it's easier than you think, as you'll see later in this chapter).

With your list in hand the next time you meet with your client, you give them a copy and a highlighter. And say:

"I'd like to help more people in _____ group. Who on this list do you think we should send [your referral kit] to?"

Notice, you're not asking them for a "referral." You're asking who you should send your kit to. This is a subtle change to the conversation most business people have, but it's very important. It changes from a taking conversation to a giving conversation.

Why Reverse Prospecting Works Like Crazy

Have you ever met anybody named "Anybody?"
Neither have your clients.

The two most commonly used words when asking for referrals usually kill your chances of getting any referrals at all. The words are "somebody" and "anybody."

They kill referrals because they are general. When you ask "Do you know anybody who needs an architect?" the little Rolodex of relationships inside your client's brain starts spinning (some reading this will be too young to know what a Rolodex is...Google it!). And usually it just keeps spinning because your client doesn't know anybody who needs an architect at that moment. So you get the, "No one comes to mind, but I'll keep my eyes open..." answer and you get **no referrals.**

Reverse prospecting is different.

You've already done the homework for them. You've figured out who they might know, who is similar enough to them that they might also need what you're selling. To be clear, you don't know if the people on the list you're about to show your client need your services or not. You've chosen them because they match your IDEAL client profile (as best as you can tell).

Now the question is different. It is specific. You've stopped the spinning Rolodex and you simply need to know who on the list they know...and who should get your referral kit.

It's a much easier task for your client because you've done the work that most business people don't do (but should). You've narrowed the universe of people down to those most likely to be IDEAL clients.

UnstoppableCEO.net

Your list isn't perfect, it never will be. But it's a heck of a lot better than no list at all.

Use Your Referral Kit to Avoid Being "Salesy"

Once your client has identified who on your list they know, simply ask who should get a copy of your referral kit. Explain that it's a gift. There's no sales pressure whatsoever. You simply want to help people understand the issues covered in your kit.

Remember your goal at this point is to open doors...to start relationships. IT IS NOT to get hot leads, ready to buy (although they will come).

If you have that posture, as if you're ready to pounce on the referrals and sell them something, it won't work. You'll scare your client and they won't make the introductions. The purity of your intent matters a great deal. If you are sincere about giving your information (your kit) with no expectation of return, you will get more introductions than you can imagine.

However, if you are simply trying to manipulate to get names, it won't work at all.

You have to let go and trust that the hot prospects will bubble up through this process. They always do. They'll be hyper-tuned to the information in your referral kit and they'll want to talk to you right away.

But you'll have a much harder time getting to them if you take a traditional, direct, referral approach.

And you'll also lose the opportunity to start relationships with many other people who will likely be hot prospects in 3, 6, 12 or 18 months.

Let's look at a couple of examples...

Case Study: Using LinkedIn (and Other Social Media) for Reverse Prospecting

In the past it might have been difficult to get the names of your client's coworkers, association colleagues or social connections.

But it's not difficult anymore...thanks to social media.

My client, John Bellino, also in financial services, uses LinkedIn to peer into his clients' networks. He can print lists of their connections, put the list in front of them and ask his client to identify who they know.

In his case, he sends a box of chocolates and a letter offering three books that describe how to create guaranteed lifetime income streams. The books are his referral kit, yet he didn't write any of them!

They are books by industry leaders.

Again, the chocolates and books are perceived as gifts.

And his clients are happy to open doors for him knowing that their colleagues will, if nothing else, appreciate the gesture of the chocolates. And, like they have, some will have a secret worry about their retirement and will find value in the books.

You could easily do the same with Facebook, Twitter and most all social media sites. They're built to connect people and to reveal those connections.

And, as John Bellino proves, you can start by creating a referral kit using someone else's books. You will, of course, want to create your own piece to gain expert positioning, but there's no reason to delay if you don't have something in place.

This is the most effective use of social media. Begging for likes and amassing "friends" you've never met is a waste of time. However, using these tools to model your REAL network of contacts and then see through it with X-Ray glasses is valuable...very valuable.

Plug into the networks of the most connected people you know...
Get The Network Infiltration Blueprint

UnstoppableCEO.net/infiltration

CHAPTER 12

How To Use Events To Create Referral Opportunities

Why Events Work So Well

Events are one of the most effective referral "kits" you can use. Just like the written kit we covered in Part 2, an event is you or your business--packaged up. It's far easier for a client to invite someone to an event you host, than to set them up for a 1-on-1 sales meeting.

And, if you look at the patterns for starting human relationships outside of business, most begin with an introduction in a group setting. There's less pressure on everyone, which allows for a *real relationship* to begin. That's what we're after...that's where the profit lives.

The most common form of referral event is the seminar. As we go through the rest of this chapter, I'll show you four ways to structure seminars, or educational events. The key to all of the most effective referral events is that they appear to be valuable education.

In fact, the easiest way to create your event presentation is to take the material in your referral kit and use it as the basis for your talk.

I prefer education over purely social events for one simple reason: In most every market, people who are willing to come to an educational talk have an interest in the topic. It's a first small and important step in qualifying real prospects, and disqualifying everyone else.

Beyond education, why do events work so well?

A live event gives you the opportunity to be face-to-face with prospects. Or, in the case of webinars and teleseminars, at least allow them to hear your voice live over the phone or Internet. This is a higher level of human bonding and can rapidly accelerate the development of trust and relationship. In other words--it's a shortcut!

Live events also position you as an expert and leader. Again, important ingredients when trying to attract the best clients and when trying to get better-than-average fees. You'll be standing at the front of the room teaching. We've been trained since age 3 or 4 to sit up straight, pay attention and grant deference and authority to the teacher at the front of the room.

That physical position literally elevates you to expert and leader before you even begin speaking--without you needing to do anything.

Because of this strong positioning and the opportunity for rapid relationship building, I often recommend events as the first step for clients who need rapid and dramatic results. Few other methods can deliver in the same way a live event can deliver.

Now, let's look at four types of live educational events. At the end of this chapter I'll also discuss the role of social events in attracting referrals.

Go Big By Going Small - How to Use Small, Private Events To Penetrate Closed Communities

We'll begin our look into the event format with small private events. These are events with just 5 to 20 guests. They work well when you're trying to penetrate closed communities of people--often found among the affluent or in certain professional groups such as doctors.

People in these communities often use the community itself as a filter to keep out shaky businesses--and only let in proven providers. That's a real challenge if you're on the outside, because it's very difficult to penetrate. Then, once you do get in, it's an enormous competitive advantage--the community filter keeps out the majority of your competition.

UnstoppableCEO.net

In these situations, you'll find it difficult to use large public events to attract these hard to reach prospects. The better approach is an intimate, private event.

The event might be a luncheon or dinner, "hosted" by your client. You sit with them, using the reverse prospecting method described in the last chapter, and together you decide who should be invited to the event and when and where to hold the event. You take care of creating the invitations and have your client either personally deliver them or you mail them under the client's signature. The invitations should appear to be personally sent by your client, whom each invitee will know well.

If your client does his job, you can expect to have virtually all those invited, attend.

Once at the event, your client will introduce you and explain why he wanted to host the event--ideally, because the work you've done for him is so great he feels that his friends and colleagues must know about it. You'll want to give an abbreviated presentation. No more than 15 to 20 minutes, with no sales pitch at the end. Simply say that you've just given them an overview and if they'd like to hear the full details that you're available to schedule a 1-on-1 appointment. The remainder of the time should be spent getting to know the attendees personally.

In my experience, 80% to 100% of the attendees will ask to meet with you.

Be sure to send everyone home with a copy of your referral kit. And add them to your regular (at least monthly) follow-up publication (more on how to create great follow-up in Part 5).

A couple of key points to consider:

1. These events work best when you create an air of exclusivity. People want desperately to be inside the velvet rope. Make the entire process from the selection of the client who will host, to the invitations, to the venue, the structure of the event and the follow-up feel exclusive.

2. The singular goal of this type of event is to start a relationship with every person invited. That's it! Do not attempt to skip ahead to the sale, you'll kill the entire feel of the event, and chances are, you'll never get your host to do another event for you. Focus on flawless execution of this step--the sales will come.

If the event is successful, the prospects will be thanking you and your client for inviting them. Think for a moment, about what those thanks mean to your client. Sure he did you a favor, but that's not the real motivation. No, the real value for the client is that he's now seen as a leader within his community of peers. The people who attended leave having higher esteem for him than when they arrived. He's gained social capital--this is extremely important to understand.

The feelings created between your client and the prospects he invited prime your client for hosting another event. If you do this type of event well, you will find that you cultivate a core group of repeat referrers. Be sure to ask again in six-months or a year--when you feel the time is right.

How One Manufacturer Uses Continuing Education to Get Referrals

Let's look at another twist on these ideas...

My client, Residential Elevators (www.residentialelevators.com), a home elevator manufacturer has a particularly challenging sales problem. They actually have three customers in every sale--the owner of the luxury home who wants an elevator, the builder and the architect designing the home (who will specify which type of elevator to use).

To reach the architects, the folks at Residential Elevators tried going direct with little success. Architects are bombarded by manufacturers of all manner of building materials and products because they hold so much control over the selection and recommendation of such products. And, as you might imagine, when faced with a continuous, frontal attack by large numbers of unwanted salespeople, the architects have developed strong defenses.

If you can't get through the front door, tunnel under the wall.

Residential Elevators found a better approach...that bypassed the "sales defenses." They created a continuing education class for architects on elevators. The architects are required to get a large number of continuing education credits each year to keep their license. Residential Elevators offers the classes to architecture firms who employ several architects. The class is free to the firm and delivered as a lunch-and-learn so everybody stays in the building.

Think about each piece of that for a moment...

The firm owners have a huge annual expense to get all of their architects the credits they need (it's customary for the firm to pay for the classes). Often, they have to send their architects away to take courses, so there's an added travel expense AND they lose all revenue the architect would have created while away at the class.

Residential Elevators removes all of those barriers...the class is offered for free, to all of the architects in the firm at the same time, on-site (no travel or lost productivity). A pretty sweet deal for the firm owner.

In return, Residential Elevators gets the undivided attention of all the architects in each firm for 60-90 minutes. They get to appear as the expert in home elevators--not a vendor. This positioning is important. Do not underestimate its worth to you. And they build relationship with the architects so the next phone call is far more likely to get through. Finally, the architects have a resource they now feel like they know and can call on the next time they need to spec out an elevator.

The course is a form of Referral Kit. When the firm owners are talking to their peers at the next association meeting they will talk about the class--and refer Residential Elevators by referring the free class.

If this all seems like a lot of work to make a sale it is...and it isn't. Most businesses use only the direct approach. Charge the front door! Charge enough doors and sooner or later you'll get through one. This is a sales approach and it works, but it's hard to sustain. You will burn through sales people with this approach. And if you're the chief sales person in your firm (which is really what the titles CEO, President, Partner and Owner mean), you'll burn yourself out.

The approach you're seeing throughout this book is a marketing approach. It's designed to build long-term relationships with people who are likely to buy what you're selling now and in the future. And it's an approach that's not only easy to sustain over the long-term...it produces greater and greater results with less effort over time.

The Secret of Seminars

Seminars are one of the most effective events for attracting referrals and for quickly turning those referrals into new clients. It is generally easy for clients and Promoters to refer people by inviting them to a seminar. It's a low-threat environment. Yet, because of the face-to-face nature of seminars and the positioning they afford you, they are one of the fastest ways to move referred prospects, even relatively cold prospects, to a sales appointment.

The structure of a typical seminar begins with 30-minutes for attendees to register and mingle. You'll want everyone who attends to sign-in so you capture their contact information for later follow-up. Having them there early, talking with one another, and with you is a key ingredient to starting the seminar successfully. Clients mix with prospects and prospects see that there are many happy clients in the room. They will ask your clients about their experience working with you. And the clients will tell them how great you are. This sells the prospect and re-sells the client on working with you and your business.

When it's time to begin the presentation have someone introduce you--give them the introduction to use, and make sure they practice it. Then begin your presentation.

You can often use your referral kit as the basis for your presentation. You'll generally want to keep the presentation to an hour, with 15-minutes at the end for questions and answers.

There are many effective ways to deliver a seminar presentation that are beyond the scope of this book. Most business people can, with reasonable practice, stand up and give a good seminar presentation about the problems their prospects face, and how they can be solved. But I do want to point out some important logistical considerations that will help you get the most value from the seminar.

Schedule Appointments In The Room

In most cases you will be using the seminar to move prospects into 1-on-1 sales meetings where you will do a needs assessment. At the end of the seminar tell the attendees that to learn how to apply the concepts you taught to their specific situation they should schedule a time to talk individually with you and that Bob or Sally or Mary from your team is at the table in the back of the room ready to set appointments.

If you've positioned it correctly, you'll have a line of people waiting to set an appointment, at every seminar.

If you skip this step and try to get them to schedule something the next day or several days later, your results will be significantly lower.

Don't Make The Food Better Than The Presentation!

For 13-years I lived in West Palm Beach, Florida. Part of the Ft. Lauderdale/Miami retirement mecca. In that area you'll see financial advisors trying to fill rooms with blue-haired grandmothers in the hopes of handling their investments and the "bait" they use to fill the room is food. They promise a steak dinner and a seminar.

And the retirees march in to get the free meal. The rooms are packed. But the retirees know that all they have to do is sit and listen and dinner's covered.

It's expensive and, in my experience, counter-productive. You want prospects to come to your seminar because they have a problem and they think they'll learn something that will help solve it. You don't want them there for the meal.

I have several clients who do seminars regularly. I do them myself, too. And we've found that some light snacks and beverages do the trick. The cost is small, usually less than $250 and you know that the people who are there are there to hear you, not eat.

How To Use A Handout

You want everyone who attends to leave with something they'll keep. Make sure they get a copy of your referral kit. And, create a handout that is designed for them to take notes on. The act of each person writing on your handout makes it his or her own. They are more likely to keep it because it has their notes. And on the handout you'll want to include your contact information.

One simple way to accomplish this is to take your outline and turn each main point into a heading or a question leaving room for notes under each section. As you move through your talk, be sure to prompt attendees to write down important points under each topic.

> Discover how one of the nation's top sales pros uses seminars to drive referrals and sales appointments (free audio).
>
> >>> UnstoppableCEO.net/ReferralResources

UnstoppableCEO.net

Webinars and Teleseminars -
Virtual Seminars

Seminars are very effective because they put you face-to-face with your prospects. If your prospects are geographically close to you it's great. But if they're spread out across your state, region, country or even around the world, getting everyone in a room isn't practical.

Instead, use a webinar or a teleseminar to allow attendees to connect to your presentation from wherever they are.

You lose the interaction between clients and prospects and you lose the face-to-face advantage, but you still have the strong expert positioning that comes with live seminars. Prospects will still hear your voice, and with some of the new video conference tools, they can see your face on their computers, too.

The key with virtual seminars is to think through the technology, from the prospect's perspective. Are they comfortable with computers? Do they regularly attend webinars? Will they have up-to-date computers to view a webinar? If you think that technology could be an issue, use a teleseminar.

A teleseminar is simply a telephone conference bridge--a special telephone number that can host dozens or hundreds of callers and allows you to deliver a talk over the phone. It's perfect in many situations, especially when technology may be an issue--most everyone has, and knows how to use, a phone.

How To Create Fast Results With A Seminar

Seminars are one of the fastest ways to jump start sales. They are relatively easy to put together and market to a local audience (more challenging if people must get on a plane to attend). And they can provide almost instant results as my client John Bellino (I introduced you to John in Chapter 11) found shortly after we began working together.

He identified a very happy client at a local university. His client's students were a mix of young people and mid-career restarts. The client felt both groups needed to hear John's message about financial and retirement security.

John scheduled two presentations: The first, for the young people, a financial 101 talk, and the second, a more advanced wealth and retirement strategy talk for the older group.

John will tell you, he's not a professional speaker. In fact, he had significant concerns about delivering both talks...concerns that we worked through and overcame.

We structured both talks to educate and leave the attendees with the conclusion that a 1-on-1 meeting was not just worth having, but urgent. John did as I recommend and had his assistant present in the room to book appointments and appointments he got!

UnstoppableCEO.net

He also, smartly, followed up with those who did not immediately book an appointment to give them a second chance. In the end he booked a number of appointments immediately. He is still, now months later, seeing a trickle of people request meetings with him as a result of the seminar. And has closed business with several in attendance and so impressed his hosts that he's already working to repeat the event.

Beyond that, John gained confidence in his abilities to deliver a successful seminar and in the model itself. When approached the right way, I've never seen it fail.

John's now working with other clients and referral partners to create a continuous string of seminars--one occurring every 4-8 weeks--with partner after partner. It has given him significant leverage in attracting prospects--now getting them a roomful at a time instead of one-by-one.

The Book Signing

If you live in a decent sized city and spend any time in a Barnes & Noble or other large bookstore, you've probably witnessed a crowd of people mobbing a table with an author sitting, smiling and signing...

Book signings are a staple of the traditional book marketing business. They work because people are drawn to the "celebrity" of an author. And, you don't have to be a famous author to get this same halo effect yourself.

The mere act of writing a book makes you "somebody." I talked about the power of books as a part of your referral kit in Part 2 of this book. Frankly, books are not that hard to create and have published, and the advantages are immense.

One such advantage is the book signing.

You don't need Barnes & Noble to "bless" your book and grant you a signing in the store. NO! Actually, far more productive for you to engineer your own book signing events. Your promoters will welcome the opportunity to position themselves within your author halo. Your celebrity, no matter how small in the grand scale of the world, is attractive. An *evening with the author* (or luncheon or whatever) is an easy event for them to promote. It's extremely benign. Not even the scent of a sales event. That's precisely what you want and why it works so well.

Your IDEAL prospects love it too. They get a 2-for-1--they get to have the "meet a celebrity" experience *and* scratch an itch related to a problem they face.

As much as I'm a fan of straight seminars, and as well as they work, they often carry the association of that Saturday "seminar" that your prospect showed up at 10 years ago that turned into a network marketing pitch they didn't want to hear. That's not a reason not to do seminars, but understand that the thought is floating in the back of the mind of nearly every prospect.

A book signing or evening with the author carries no such baggage. And the positioning it affords is greater than just about any other event you can create. The word "authority" begins with "author." You get both author and speaker authority, instead of one or the other.

The act of signing your book for attendees, having them stand in line to get your signature, to speak with you is all theater for the subconscious. A carefully choreographed development of the image of you being someone of importance.

Now, I don't know about you, but my mother raised me to believe that bragging, self-aggrandizement and boasting were behaviors to avoid. And you may be thinking after reading the preceding paragraphs that it all sounds highly egotistical. To a degree it is. Frankly, it is something I'm still not used to. It takes me out of my comfort zone and it will likely do the same for you. It's OK.

The truth that mother never told us was this...in business, no one else is going to blow your horn. You've got to get comfortable blowing it yourself, or *arranging* ways to have others blow it. Either way, you're driving the bus...you are the chief promoter of your business. Comfortable or not, it must be done.

The book signing is a way for others to blow the horn for you. It's critical that you understand the psychological and emotional motives of the people who attend such an event. The things I described above, summarized as "rubbing elbows with someone important" are desired by the prospects that show up. Do not disappoint. You cheat them and you.

The format for a book signing is slightly different than the seminar. You'll want your Promoter to introduce you. Write the introduction for them!

Give a short 20-30 minute talk. Sign books. Mingle with people. Have someone there with your calendar to schedule appointments with you.

You can either give away your books or sell them. And you can get creative with this as you'll see in the next example.

Case Study: How To Get The United Way To Host Your Book Signing

Client and friend John Curry, mentioned elsewhere in this book is a master of marketing choreography in his own right. As a part of the launch of his book--*The Secure Retirement Method* –John struck a partnership with the local United Way organization.

He offered to sell the book for its list price of $20 a copy and donate all the money to the United Way. In return, the local CEO of the United Way helped promote the book signing and was on hand to introduce John...and gave a powerful introduction to-boot!

UnstoppableCEO.net

John used the association with the United Way in his own marketing, creating affinity with many in the community who support the charity's mission. The donation of the book proceeds demonstrated purity of intent and built trust. Done sincerely, with the trust benefits being a welcome by-product.

As a part of the promotion he created a poster with his photo, the book cover and the United Way logo. The poster now hangs in his office, viewed over his left shoulder by clients and prospects in 1-on-1 meetings...providing long-term credibility, authority, trust and prestige from this single event.

Note the number of ways this event has been used and reused. And that's just one book signing.

Similar events can be done, with or without charity ties, as partnerships with associations, promoters or civic groups. The concept can be paired with the small seminars described earlier in this chapter, creating intimate evening with the author events.

The opportunities available to you with a book as a referral device are not available at all without a book. It is an easy and valuable way to open doors with prospects. And most businesses who use books in their marketing will tell you that their best, highest profit customers are those who read their books.

This is an investment approach.

The "sales approach" is a consumption approach...you eat tonight what you killed today.

Both work, but only one scales.

Some Thoughts on Parties

Everybody loves a party. And there are plenty of reason to throw a party for business.

Yet, I question their effectiveness in driving a consistent flow of qualified referrals. The reason--people attend parties to be social. That's the motivating factor. They attend seminars, workshops, evenings with the author primarily because of the promise of discovering a solution to a problem they have.

That's a more qualified and valuable prospect.

Parties and social events have their place...for fun, for fellowship, and for deepening existing relationships with clients and Promoters. And you can successfully use social events to open new referral relationships. However, in my experience they are never as productive as information-centric events.

So, use them, but understand their role as relationship development or deepening, not necessarily as prospect attraction or qualification.

Part Five:
Growing Referrals
Into Clients

CHAPTER 13

The Most Predictable Business Growth Model Ever Discovered

What we've discussed so far is what I call "opening doors." It is the first and necessary part of the most predictable business growth model ever discovered. Master the techniques I've covered up-to-now and you'll have no shortage of new leads and you'll have a system for continually getting them.

But it is only the first piece of the puzzle.

The second, necessary, piece is what happens next. You've delivered your referral kit, or interviewed partners who've shared you with their audience or hosted a successful seminar or book signing. Great!

Now what?

You've opened lots of doors. Some saw you at the door and welcomed you in, asking for immediate help. But the majority greeted you, listened to your message and did nothing.

Does that mean they are somehow poor prospects?

Not at all. If they responded by requesting your referral kit or attending your event you know they perceive a need for your help on some level. But for one of any number of reasons, today is not the day for them to buy. That's OK. You have successfully planted a seed for future harvest. Author and business expert Dan Kennedy calls this "future bank." The prospects who become clients today are your "present bank." They pay you, and you use the money, largely, to pay today's bills to support today's life needs.

Most companies market only to fill the present bank. Yet at very small cost, they could plant the seeds of future sales--making deposits in their future bank--by simply staying in touch with the unconverted leads.

Most do not. And you should be glad. The void they leave is opportunity for you.

In this last section of the book, I'm going to show you how to take what you've already created and use it to build a perpetual, welcomed, valuable follow-up system that will build your future bank.

Open Lots Of Doors

The first part of the most predictable business growth model ever discovered is to open lots of doors. Many more than you've likely opened before. This is radically different then the typical 1-by-1 referral model. The old model simply doesn't scale. It requires essentially the same amount of effort (sometimes more) to develop a single referral using the old model as it does to develop 5 or 10 or 100 using the methods described in this book.

Most business owners I meet grossly underestimate the number of new relationships they must open each day, week, month and year to maintain predictable growth. And most make it difficult to open a door with a prospect. Often the one and only commitment offered a prospect is to buy.

Sure that's the end goal, but it ignores the vast majority of prospects. Remember, you have only 2%-3% of the market who know they have a need, are actively looking for a solution and are ready to buy when they find it. Three-percent...tops!

So in your prospecting and referral work, that means that three people out of every one-hundred are ready to become your client today. An additional 7% are open to the idea of buying and an additional 30% aren't thinking about it...yet, but might be open to the idea.

Your opportunity is with the 7% that are open to buying now and the 30% who aren't thinking about buying, but might be interested. This second group likely perceives a need, but either isn't fully aware of it yet or it has not become a priority for them...but odds are it will become a priority.

So let's break this down. If you're focused on opening as many doors as possible, you're going to attract your share of the 2%-3% who are ready today. At least as many as you could get using the old 1-by-1 methods. And, in addition you're going to open doors--start relationships--with many in the next 7% who are open to the idea of buying. If you stopped right there, you have taken your universe of potential prospects from 3% to as much as 10% of the market--more than triple.

But don't stop there. If you use, as I've suggested throughout this book, opening offers that require little more than the exchange of contact information to get your referral kit or attend your event--very low barriers to jump over--you will find that you also attract many from the 30% who aren't thinking about buying now, but somewhere, in the back of their mind, perceive a need. Even if it's a distant need.

You've planted a seed. It's now up to you, to grow that seed of a relationship into a client.

And your future fortune, business stability and long-term wealth depend on it.

How to Create Great Buyers

The best clients--IDEAL clients--have one thing in common. They are educated about your product or service. If you really want to be successful, you only want to deal with educated buyers--as long as you're the one who educated them.

When educated properly (**by you**), they have greater trust, which is necessary to make the sale. They are more compliant because they trust you, meaning they will defer to your recommendations and expertise. And maybe most important, they are generally not price motivated. They've been educated to understand that value is more important than price. This is not the only way to sell at higher than market prices, but it's the most predictable and stable.

Three Reasons You'll *Want* To Educate Prospects

#1. **Done right, your educational marketing will set the buying criteria in the mind of the prospect.** Let me explain. One of my consulting clients is a roofing contractor. They face stiff competition, often from "pickup truck" operators who run their business out of their garage and the back of a pickup truck. My client is one of the top companies in the Southeast, with reputation and overhead to match. They can't and don't want to compete with the guy working out of his truck with no overhead. It's a price battle they can't win. But they offer a lot for a homeowner beyond nailing shingles to the roof--added value.

If they don't take the time to educate a homeowner on the importance and value of those "extras," then the homeowner only has one criteria to use in making a decision--price.

For my client, we developed a 24-page report for homeowners. They get it before my client meets with them. And in the report it sets a number of buying criteria designed to make the guy in the truck a non-competitor. In fact, we even point out that my client has a nice showroom, that's been in the same location for over a decade--you, Mr. Homeowner can find us if you have a problem with your roof. Versus, the guy in the truck--if he decides to ignore your calls you have no way to find him. He has no office.

This is not just a made up risk. My client has come in behind these types of competitors to fix messes when they've disappeared before completing the roof (even though they got all the money). We're simply taking reality and explaining to the buyer that it exists and why it's important to them.

#2. You communicate your advantages in the context of education, not selling. By providing education before you engage in selling to the prospect, you make it easier for your point of view to be accepted. Imagine my roofing client sitting in your living room with a contract on the table for you to buy a new roof and telling you the same story about the "pickup truck" guy. Hearing it at that point makes you skeptical, right?

It has the appearance of being self-serving because the roofer has something to gain immediately if you believe the story. That immediate conflict of interest causes doubt and erodes the credibility of the information. Even though the information is still real, relevant and valuable.

Much more effective to communicate your advantages before you're in the sales conversation. They then become assumed fact by the time you enter the sales conversation. Nice to have a prospect take all of your advantages and assume them to be fact before you ever try to sell them anything, 'eh!

#3. Education Without Obligation Breeds Trust. When you give away something like your referral kit, you are offering to educate prospects without any obligation that they do business with you. It's a *demonstration* that you care about their outcome more than your gain. Most businesses say they're about client outcomes first. And I believe that most really are. But if everybody's saying it, prospects aren't likely to believe it. So don't say it-- demonstrate it.

Education Doesn't Happen Overnight

It takes time to educate a prospect prior to making a complex, high-dollar buying decision. Most fail to account for the time needed for education. They focus on the prospects who are ready to buy today, and live by "sales tricks" to pull their share of today's buyers over the

UnstoppableCEO.net

finish line. If all you do is focus on the ready-to-buy prospects you're going to have to deal with price competition much more often than you should. Your buyers simply haven't been taught to value other things more than price.

This is foolish. You can and should control the buyer's perception and thinking around price. Most buyers want some other indicator, search for some other indicator that they are making the right decision. Why not give them what they want?

If you begin to look at prospects in the 7% and the first 30% tier that Chet Holmes described. Prospects that are either likely to buy, but aren't quite ready and prospects who would be open to the idea of buying. If you understand that there is virtually no competition for these prospects--everybody is focused on killing today so they can eat tonight. If you focus on opening doors with prospects in these two groups and educating them over time, until they are ready, you'll find that your business becomes much more stable, predictable and profitable.

Why You Must Take The Long View

The buying cycle for high-dollar products and services is almost always longer than you're aware of. Prospects start with a tiny nagging thought that there's a problem. Unless the problem is, for some external reason, elevated to crisis level, that nagging thought will take time to grow.

As it does, the prospect will seek out information to help understand the nature of the problem. To find out who else experiences the problem. To learn about possible cures for the problem. And ultimately to find a source for the cure.

Business-to-business or business-to-consumer-- doesn't matter, the process is the same. And the process happens over time. Some prospects go through these steps in a day, others may take a year or more. You can't control the pace they travel. You can, however, match your marketing to this process of discovery your prospects are following.

It's easy to stay with the prospect whose buying process happens in a day or a week or even a month. But the majority will take longer. Yet, few businesses account for the long buying cycle. Few have a plan to systematically educate, build trust and develop relationship with a prospect over 6-months, a year or more.

This fact creates a huge opportunity for you. To illustrate the point here are sales follow-up statistics from a McGraw-Hill study of 10,000 businesses across all industries.

- **48% of sales people never follow up with a prospect**
- 25% of sales people make a second contact and stop

- 12% of sales people make three contacts and stop
- Only 10% of sales people make more than three contacts
- Only 2% of sales are made on the first contact
- Just 3% of sales are made on the second contact
- 5% of sales are made on the third contact
- 10% of sales are made on the fourth contact
- *Fully 80% of sales are made on the 5th to 12th contact*

Note the two most important numbers: Only 10% of sales people make more than three contacts and 80% of sales are made on the 5th to 12th contact.

What that means is that 90% of the competition drops out before 80% of the sales are going to be made. Leaving that 80% for just 10% of the companies to compete over. Pretty good odds in my book...how about yours?

The reason most drop out is that follow-up is, quite frankly, boring and requires thought and work. Most people, business owners included, are averse to both. What they don't know, and what you will find out in the next chapter is that there are shortcuts that make follow-up very easy.

Putting the Pieces Together

This chapter is titled "The Most Predictable Business Growth Model Ever Discovered" and as you've seen here and throughout this book, the model is simple. It has two parts--open lots of doors to new relationships and educate those people until they are ready to become your client.

When you build it as I've described you'll find that new clients will "bubble up" when they're ready. When they do, selling isn't necessary. They already know you, like you and trust you...your educational marketing created that in them. They know what to value when making the buying decision and understand why they should pay you a premium.

In short order, you'll see a ratio emerge between the number of doors you open and the number of new clients you get 3-months, 6-months and 12-months in the future. You will be able to predict, with astonishing accuracy, what your business growth will look like at specific points in the future.

By focusing on the simple "door opening" strategies I shared in this book you can create many more opportunities to open doors to new client relationships, while investing less time and effort than if you use the old 1-by-1 referral approach. And you can eliminate the up and down roller coaster of sales that exists in most businesses.

At the same time, your continued "marketing" to existing clients, in the form of the interview strategy I shared in Part 3 serves as a fence around your existing clients, keeping them always engaged with you--not looking with a wandering eye at one of your competi-tors.

In the next chapter you'll discover how to build easy, endless and valuable follow-up to get the most out of every door you open.

Discover the essential tools I recommend to private consulting clients to automate and streamline their referral marketing...

UnstoppableCEO.net/ReferralResources

CHAPTER 14

Fabulously Effective Follow-up in 90-Minutes a Month

The Three Essential Elements of Every Follow-up Touch

Most of the follow-up efforts I come across fail because they're completely one-sided...they're all about the company trying to sell you something. It leaves out all the romance. There's nothing there to warm you up. Big mistake and easily corrected.

Good follow-up needs to do three things:

1. Entertain. People pay attention to what entertains them. You have a continuously running example of this in your living room right now...turn on the TV. The entertainment pieces exist for one reason and one reason only. To get you to sit there, in front of that box so the TV station can show you advertisements. And they've figured out that if they just run the ads 24/7 you're not likely to watch. So they give you the ads, with "a spoonful of sugar," knowing that you'll sit there and tolerate the ads if you're entertained. Prospects are getting so discerning that big brands are moving from 30 or 60-second stand-alone commercials to in-show product placement to make the commercial messages more palatable.

Same deal with magazines. So ask yourself, "Why would marketing my business be any different?" Your prospects are human, they LIKE to be entertained. Even CEOs of big companies LIKE to be entertained. I'm not saying you need to turn your marketing into a comedy act, but figure out how to weave some entertainment into it.

2. **Be Valuable.** Every message you put in front of a prospect must be valuable to the prospect. And they define what's valuable. Usually, you're going to be valuable by delivering education on the problem they're facing, that you solve. The information you deliver must really be beneficial and not simply an offer to buy.

You want your prospects to know that anything they get from you is going to be so good, that they'll stop what they're doing, open it, sit and read it immediately.

3. **Offer a Clear Next Step.** If you've entertained and delivered value and done it consistently, you'll have a percentage of prospects who are ready to move forward

after each follow-up piece. That's great, it's what you want. Now you need to give them a next step. What is the next logical step they should take to solve their problem?

Is it to schedule a 1-on-1 needs assessment? Buy an entry-level product? Attend a seminar or webinar?

Whatever that next step is, make sure you put it in every follow-up piece, so the prospects who are ready know how to get closer to the solution they need.

There are two ways to make your offer:

#1 - Make a direct offer. Direct offers explicitly tell the prospect what they should do next--for example, "call xxx-xxx-xxxx to schedule a free financial physical" (a euphemism for "sales meeting").

#2 - A low-key offer. A low-key offer is one in which you insert the offer for the next step into the content of the follow-up piece so that it appears to be a part of the normal flow. In other words, it's not blatant and direct. I regularly use low-key offers in my daily email newsletter *The Unstoppable CEO™ Online* (UnstoppableCEO.net/online).

In case you didn't notice, that's an example of a low-key next step offer. If you want to see how I mix content, entertainment and both direct and low-key offers, you really should subscribe to *The Unstoppable CEO™ Online.* It's a real shortcut for learning how to master these offers. Go to UnstoppableCEO.net/online to get your free subscription. (And yes, that's a direct offer...go now...get it!)

What's the Frequency?

What's the perfect follow-up frequency? It's a lot more frequent than you think.

When most people start to think about follow-up frequency they default to quarterly. Don't bother. Three-months is way too long for a prospect to go without hearing from you. You might as well not follow-up at all.

I recommend monthly at a minimum. And if you're truly hitting all three of the elements I discussed in the last section--entertainment, value and a clear next step--frequent communication will be welcomed by your prospects.

In fact, I've found that the higher the frequency the better--weekly and even daily communication work very well. Here's why...

Your best prospects not only want information about their problem and the solution you offer, they are also developing a relationship with "you"--your business. They want a relationship with the people in your business. Usually this means the business owner (even in very large companies--think Apple/Steve Jobs, Virgin/Richard Branson and Berkshire-Hathaway/Warren Buffet).

Do this well, and they'll pay attention to what you send them because they simply want to know what you think about a particular topic.

They'll feel as though they know you. I have this experience regularly enough that I know it's a real phenomenon--people who read my own daily newsletter (UnstoppableCEO.net/online) will email me as if we're friends, or come up to me at conferences and speak as though they've known me for years. And in a sense they have known me for years through the messages I send.

I have a relationship with them, yet I've never met them. That last little fact doesn't diminish the quality of the relationship at all. It exists in their mind and that's just fine. The fact that you or I can develop that kind of strong bond in another person's mind, without ever meeting them by simply staying in touch and being valuable to them frequently is a breakthrough for most businesses.

Think for a moment about the people in your life with whom you have the strongest relationships. I'll bet you have contact with all of them at least once a month. Most weekly. And daily with the most important people in your life.

And the people you only hear from every few months, or only at Christmas...they're in your life, but not usually all that important. Don't try to buck human nature--harness it.

Why You're Too Chicken To
Follow-up Frequently

Ok, here's why you'll read this and still not do it. We may as well be honest about it...

You're afraid you'll make somebody mad or annoyed and then they won't buy from you. Yes, it's a real risk, but a VERY small one.

When I switched from sending an email newsletter every other week to every weekday, I was told that I'd have half of my subscribers drop-out in the first week. And that I'd lose subscribers in greater numbers as time went on.

It never happened. When I announced the switch in frequency, less than 1% dropped their subscriptions. And over the last 18 months I've sent over 250 emails. During that time, the average number of opt-outs per week is lower than it was when I mailed less frequently.

People want relationship. They want leadership. You can't give them either if you're not showing up in their lives on a regular basis.

Will some find your follow-up to be too much...even offensive? Yes. They're not ever going to be clients anyway. Better to know that now, than to waste resources on them for years.

So the perfect frequency...

If you're thinking quarterly, forget it, you might as well not send anything. By the time they get each quarterly touch, they'll have forgotten you. You force yourself to start over with every contact. You want to think of follow-up as a continuing conversation with your prospects and clients. Would you go for a a whole quarter without talking to the most important people in your life? Probably not.

The minimum you should be doing is monthly communication. And if you do monthly, you'll want to send something more memorable than an email. The goal isn't just the touch, you want impact and attention, without which you can't get them to take a next step towards buying.

Monthly is minimum, and I advise my private clients to, if at all possible, engineer a reason to show up weekly...even several times a week or daily.

There is a direct correlation between increased sales and increased frequency.

Leveraging The Content You Already Have

If you're using interviews as I've described, as a means to get access to Promoters then you've already solved the most significant impediment most business owners face when doing follow-up--coming up with all the content.

You'll have new content each time you do an interview of a Promoter. Choose your interviews well and you'll have great fodder for your monthly, weekly or even daily follow-up. You can publish the interviews in audio or in print, it really doesn't matter.

Done well, with disguised promotional wrappers for your business, you not only have very compelling content, but you also have *sales opportunities* with each follow-up touch.

There's so much money left sitting on the table from poor follow-up that you're nuts if you don't fix this in your business.

CHAPTER 15

How to Know if You're Succeeding at Attracting Referrals

You'll see an increase in prospects referred to you and converted into clients. The numbers will show you. And the turn is often swift, with a boost in new referrals occurring in the first days and weeks after you begin applying the methods I've described.

Long-term, with consistent application of these methods, you will see an ever growing "pool of prospects" and from that growing pool, a predictable and consistently increasing number of new clients. If you've experienced and up and down revenue cycle before, you'll find that the peaks and valleys smooth out to give you an even growth curve.

You'll also find that as word spreads among the groups of Promoters you wish to work with, that promoters will begin to seek you out. As this happens you'll find that you can accelerate your referral machine with less and less effort on your part.

This is the goal.

We are aiming to ease the acquisition of great clients. More with less effort. That is the essence of the methods in this book.

Just remember the two very important parts of the system—opening doors and growing clients.

You can open lots of doors very quickly with the methods I explain in Parts Two and Three of this book. Yet, if you do not follow-through and grow those new relationships into clients you'll likely be disappointed with your results. The systematic methods for staying in front of and developing relationship with prospects, described in Part Four, is the secret sauce to this formula.

With all the parts together, you have a simple to implement, ever expanding way to attract referrals...and you won't ever need to create the feeling of stress in yourself and your clients that comes with the old referral model.

Discover the Secret *"Network Infiltration Blueprint"* and Easily Tap-Into the Networks of the Most Connected People You Know

A good friend of mine likes to say, there are only two kinds of prospects—*those you know, and those you don't know.* Pretty simple and quite profound.

Most business owners struggle their entire career trying to attract prospects they don't know. Spending tens of thousands of dollars on advertising. Wasting hundreds of hours each year attending "networking" events that seldom yield results. Going to expensive and time-consuming tradeshows hoping to land enough new clients to make a return. And all of it is unnecessary.

You're sitting on an untapped well of prospects you don't know…hidden from your view and waiting to be accessed. You just need to know how to drill down and find them.

My new guide—**The Network Infiltration Blueprint™ (over $200 value)**—will show you step-by-step, how to infiltrate the networks of the most connected people you know and turn prospects you don't know into ones you know *and* who know you.

This is the fastest way I know to unlock the power profit lying hidden inside your network.

The Network Infiltration Blueprint is available exclusively to subscribers to my monthly business intelligence briefing for successful CEOs—The Unstoppable CEO™ CONFIDENTIAL.

Subscribe today and I'll rush your copy of the The Network Infiltration Blueprint™ to you by First Class Mail.

UnstoppableCEO.net/Infiltration

Free Resources

Go to UnstoppableCEO.net/ReferralResources to access free resources for book owners, including:

- ✓ An interview with one of the top salesmen in the world on how he attracts referrals for hard-to-sell products and services.
- ✓ The 10-minute Referability Assessment – identify how to increase your referability.
- ✓ Downloadable templates you can use to attract referrals right away.
- ✓ The latest research and methods for attracting more referrals with less effort.
- ✓ Recordings of referral marketing presentations by Steve Gordon.
- ✓ A complete guide to the tools you need to build your referral marketing system.
- ✓ …and much more!

UnstoppableCEO.net/ReferralResources

Steve Gordon Speaking, Consulting and Copywriting Availability

Mr. Gordon has limited availability for new speaking and marketing consulting engagements. To have Steve speak to your group, either at your event or via webinar to your members, go to UnstoppableCEO.net/SpeakingInquiry.

All consulting and copywriting engagements begin with a Discovery Call. For Discovery Call availability and to schedule an appointment, go to UnstoppableCEO.net/ConsultingApplication.

ABOUT THE AUTHOR

Steve Gordon became CEO of his first company at age 28. He's invested the last 20 years in the study and application of selling high-ticket services. He is the editor of four business newsletters read by thousands of CEOs, professional practitioners, entrepreneurs and sales pros around the world. Steve consults with businesses in 30 different industries, all selling high-ticket products and services in high-trust selling environments. He lives in Tallahassee, Florida with his wife Erin and their four children.

Connect with Steve at UnstoppableCEO.net and listen to **free behind-the-scenes interviews with successful CEOs of small and mid-size companies**...Discover how they found success and apply the lessons they learned to your business.

24824986R00100

Made in the USA
San Bernardino, CA
07 October 2015